On the cover:

**Masqueraders at Mi-Carême in Chéticamp around 1945.**
(Centre culturel Les Trois Pignons Collection)

# Acadian Mi-Carême

For Tish,

A book that will certainly bring back fond memories.

Enjoy!

Georges Arsenault

19 April 2009

Georges Arsenault

# Acadian Mi-Carême
## *Masks and Merrymaking*

Translated by Sally Ross


**The Acorn Press**
Charlottetown
2009

**ISBN 978-1-894838-40-5**



Edited by Laurie Brinklow

Cover and book design by Raymond Thériault

Printed in Canada by Hignell Book Printing

The publisher acknowledges the support of the Government of Canada through the Book Publishing Industry Development Program (BPIDP) of the Department of Canadian Heritage for our publishing activities. We also acknowledge the support of the Canada Council for the Arts and the Prince Edward Island Department of Communities, Cultural Affairs, and Labour for our publishing program.

*Acadian Mi-Carême: Masks and Merrymaking* first appeared in French as *La Mi-Carême en Acadie*, published by Éditions La Grande Marée, Tracadie-Sheila, New Brunswick, 2007.

**Library and Archives Canada Cataloguing in Publication**

Arsenault, Georges, 1952–
Acadian mi-carême: masks and merrymaking / Georges Arsenault; translator, Sally Ross.

Translation of: La mi-carême en Acadie.
Includes bibliographical references.
ISBN 978-1-894838-40-5

1. Winter festivals—Maritime Provinces—History. 2. Acadia—Social life and customs. 3. Maritime Provinces—Social life and customs. I. Ross, Sally II. Title.

GT4503.15.A7813 2009 394.2509715 C2009-900161-6

ACORNPRESS

P.O. Box 22024
Charlottetown, Prince Edward Island C1A 9J2
acornpresscanada.com

# Contents

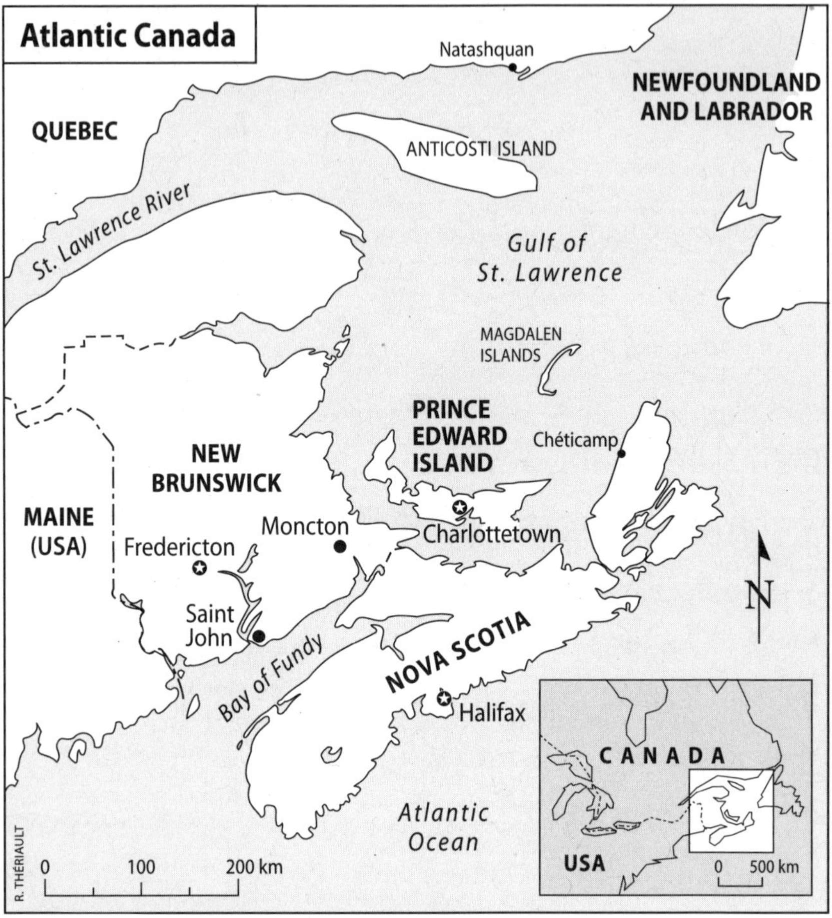
Atlantic Canada
Natashquan
NEWFOUNDLAND AND LABRADOR
QUEBEC
ANTICOSTI ISLAND
St. Lawrence River
Gulf of St. Lawrence
MAGDALEN ISLANDS
PRINCE EDWARD ISLAND
Chéticamp
NEW BRUNSWICK
MAINE (USA)
Moncton
Fredericton
Charlottetown
Saint John
Bay of Fundy
NOVA SCOTIA
Halifax
Atlantic Ocean
N
CANADA
USA
0 100 200 km
0 500 km
R. THÉRIAULT

## Other Maps

# Acknowledgements

I would like express my sincerest thanks to all the people who in one way or another contributed to the preparation of this book. First of all, I would like to thank the personnel at the following institutions that gave me access to their collections: the Centre d'études acadiennes at the Université de Moncton, the Centre acadien at the Université Sainte-Anne, the Archives de folklore et d'ethnologie at the Université Laval, the Canadian Museum of Civilization, the Centre de la Mi-Carême in Saint-Joseph-du-Moine, and Les Trois Pignons in Chéticamp.

Many individuals from the Acadian areas of Nova Scotia, New Brunswick, Prince Edward Island, and Quebec kindly answered my questions about Mi-Carême, either in the form of an interview or a questionnaire. I am most grateful to all of them.

Numerous people contributed to my research by accepting to share their manuscripts or the results of their surveys or by looking for photographs or by giving me the names of possible informants. In particular, I would like to thank Monique Aucoin, Fernand Arsenault, Corinne Arsenault, Guy Côté, Kenneth Breau, Carmen d'Entremont, Sébastien Dol, Michelle Deraspe, Jean-Claude Dupont, Bérangère Landry, Bernard Landry, Angus Lefort, Lauraine Léger, Jean-Pierre Pichette, Rita Poirier, Robert Richard, Marie-Colombe Robichaud, and Charlie Dan Roach.

I would also like to express my thanks to Denise Paquette for her wonderful illustrations and to Mylène Ouellette for transcribing the tunes of the Mi-Carême songs.

I am profoundly grateful to a number of good friends who kindly accepted to read and correct my original manuscript in French. My special thanks go to Marielle Cormier-Boudreau, Ronald Labelle, Monique Lafontaine, Barbara LeBlanc, and Sally Ross for their invaluable help.

My thanks also go to the graphic designer Raymond Thériault who created a wonderful "costume" for my book on Acadian Mi-Carême, and to the translator Sally Ross who captured a friendly and credible English voice for the many aspects of Mi-Carême.

I would like to thank the Canada Council for the Arts which provided the translation grant. Finally, I would like to express my sincerest gratitude to Laurie Brinklow and The Acorn Press for making *La Mi-Carême en Acadie* available in English. I sincerely hope that this book will help bring new life to the very old and colourful Acadian customs of Mi-Carême.

Georges Arsenault

# Preface

*According to the Acadian tradition, the word "Mi-Carême" (a feminine noun) has four different meanings: 1) the day in the middle of Lent when the festivities take place; 2) any person wearing a mask and costume who participates in the festivities; 3) the mythical woman who brings gifts and sometimes even babies; and 4) the scary character who comes and takes children away if they misbehave.*

Whenever I think of the Mi-Carême or Mid-Lent celebrations of my childhood, they conjure up the smell of mothballs and the old clothes my mother stored away carefully in the attic. These clothes were eventually used to make blankets and rugs, and sometimes even items of clothing for the younger members of the family. In the meantime, however, little balls of naphthalene protected the outdated wardrobe from hungry moths, but not from the hands of anyone rummaging for the makings of a costume for Mi-Carême. As soon as I got home from school on the day of Mi-Carême (the fourth Thursday of Lent), I would race up to the attic to find a disguise of some sort, whether it was a wrinkled old dress, a coat full of holes, or a long cotton stocking to be quickly converted into a mask. In a few minutes, I had all the makings of my disguise and was ready to put on my costume. I do not recall ever having thought about washing anything to get rid of the smell of naphthalene. There was no time to waste, especially since automatic washing machines and electric clothes dryers had not yet arrived in Abram-Village. In any case, the smell of moth balls was not going to deter me from making the rounds of our neighbourhood on Mi-Carême.

I have wonderful memories of this wintertime masquerade that I enjoyed, along with a neighbour the same age as me, and sometimes with one or two of my sisters. We never went far. We only visited our closest neighbours who knew us very well. Sometimes they would give us a cookie or a piece of fudge, but we never expected to get a treat at every house. The aim was not to be recognized by our hosts. They would ask us questions like: "Does the Mi-Carême live far from here? What's her name? Can she dance?" And, of course, we would disguise our voices, perform a few dance steps, and pound on the floor with our canes.

By the mid-1960s, fewer and fewer people were disguising themselves and going visiting on Mi-Carême in my native village. When I returned to Prince Edward Island in 1977, after finishing my studies at university, I soon discovered that the celebration of Mi-Carême had all but disappeared. It saddened me to think that this ancient custom was going to be lost forever. I was eager to see it come alive again. So I got together with a few of my friends and, for several years, we had fun going from house to house, hoping to bring back memories for those who knew the tradition of Mi-Carême and to show it to young people who had never had the opportunity to witness it, let alone take part in it. I even took pen in hand and wrote an article for the Acadian weekly newspaper *La Voix acadienne*, in the hope of inspiring readers to revive the customs associated with Mi-Carême in their own village. With tongue in cheek, I asked what had become of our beloved Mi-Carême:

> Is it possible that she's only interested in modern pleasures and that she's lost the desire to go visiting? That's hard to believe. I can't see our Mi-Carême playing Bingo every other night or sprawled out in front of the television watching *Another World* or *The Price is Right*. No, that's not possible! The Mi-Carême I know has too much fun running around the community to become a slave to Bingo or TV.[1]

1. Georges Arsenault, "La Mi-Carême est-elle droguée?", *La Voix acadienne*, 22 February 1978, p. 8; also published in *Le Courrier de la Nouvelle-Écosse*, 2 March 1978, p. 3.

**Posing for posterity.** In 1979, on the initiative of Georges Arsenault (under the clock), this group of Mi-Carêmes visited several households in the Evangeline region of Prince Edward Island. (Georges Arsenault Collection)

Unfortunately, I did not succeed in reviving the Acadian tradition of Mid-Lent, at least not as I had known it in my youth. I might have inspired a few individuals to disguise themselves and to go from door to door, especially to visit elderly people. But my efforts were not far-reaching enough to affect children or teenagers who, for the most part, had never had the privilege of meeting a Mi-Carême in person.

However, I have never lost interest in this traditional festivity. During the fifteen years that I hosted the Prince Edward Island Radio-Canada morning radio show, I made sure that Mi-Carême never went unnoticed. On several occasions, we were actually able to broadcast live from Acadian community centres, surrounded by listeners and, of course, by a few lively masked visitors.

This book is obviously a logical continuation of my efforts to preserve the memory of this venerable tradition, to make it better known, and even to bring it back to life. When I was doing my research in the Maritimes and the Acadian communities in the province of Québec, I was both surprised and thrilled to see how extraordinarily popular this Acadian custom once was and, in many cases, still is. I was fascinated to discover that our Mi-Carême played several roles and that she might even have brought me into this world! If that be true, as a sign of my gratitude, it is with pleasure that I dedicate this book to her.

# A Rich and Varied Tradition

Memories of Mi-Carême or Mid-Lent are still very much alive in many Acadian areas. For some people, they go back to their childhood. For others, they are associated with recent events in their own communities. People still put on their masks and costumes to go visiting for the annual Mi-Carême celebrations in Chéticamp and Saint-Joseph-du-Moine in Cape Breton, Nova Scotia; in Fatima on the Magdalen Islands; in Natashquan and Pointe-Parent on the North Shore of Quebec; and in the Tignish and Palmer Road area of Prince Edward Island.

Mi-Carême or Demi-Carême, as it is known in some Acadian regions, was one of those anticipated pleasures that broke the monotony of the long winter months. Coming after Christmas, New Year's, Epiphany, Candlemas, and Mardi Gras (Shrove Tuesday), it was the last feast day of winter. Mi-Carême was greeted even more enthusiastically because it fell in the middle of Lent, the period of seven weeks of strict fasting, penance, and mortification preceding Easter, which the Catholic Church imposed on the faithful. Mi-Carême is celebrated on the fourth Thursday of Lent. Like Easter, it is a movable feast so it takes place on a different date every year sometime between 26 February and 1 April.[2]

Many people took advantage of Mi-Carême to "break" Lent, in other words to take a break from their penitences and even indulge in such things as card games, music, dancing, sweets,

---

2. See: univ-lemans.fr/~hainry/tableaux/tabl5.html. Between 1801 and 2000, Mi-Carême fell on 26 February in 1818 only, and on 1 April in 1886 and in 1943.

and other foods that one had to give up for Lent. And, of course, there was the annual masquerade of the mummers or Mi-Carêmes who went visiting from house to house. As Éveline Chiasson says, it was a chance to let off a little steam: "By the end of the fourth week of Lent, it was time to get moving and let loose a bit. We weren't too keen on that period of penance that seemed to go on forever. So we seized the opportunity to take a break."[3]

As we shall see, the rich and varied traditions associated with Mi-Carême were firmly anchored in the folkways of Acadian communities. Mi-Carême was a time for making house-visits in groups, but there was also the mysterious person, called the Mi-Carême, who distributed candies to little children or sometimes even delivered babies and animals. For many young Acadians, however, this strange individual was a scary character who could come and take them away if they misbehaved.

These traditions were not invented on this side of the Atlantic. On the contrary, they were common in France, especially in Brittany and Normandy. After crossing the ocean with the early settlers, they became well-established in the New World, as evidenced by the fact that they were practised enthusiastically in almost every Acadian region until the 1960s and are still alive today in some communities.

3. Éveline Chiasson, *Ma mère et moi. Au coeur de notre famille acadienne.* Bas-Caraquet: Éditions du Goéland, 1998, p. 89.

# Lent

The institution of Lent dates back to the birth of Christianity, although for a number of centuries it was of no fixed duration. By the beginning of the Middle Ages, however, Lent was limited to forty weekdays and six Sundays of fasting. During this period of forty-six days, which began on Ash Wednesday and ended on Holy Saturday, it was forbidden to eat meat or other animal products such as milk, cheese, and eggs.[4] All Roman Catholics were obliged to follow this regime — to not do so was considered sinful. According to Father Philias F. Bourgeois, even as late as the mid-1800s, Acadians "did not eat any foods other than potatoes, fish and buckwheat bread" during Lent.[5]

For many centuries, Lent was a period of strict abstinence, but the Catholic Church gradually began making concessions. In 1703, the First Ritual of the Diocese of Quebec (which included Acadie) lifted the obligation to fast from "individuals who were not yet twenty-one years of age; decrepit and crippled elderly people over the age of sixty; wet nurses; pregnant women; valetudinarians; those who undertake long and painful journeys; or those who are unable to work without seriously damaging their health."[6] Two centuries later, Lent was still very demanding, but it was no longer as strict. Meat was even allowed on certain days. In 1894, the newspaper

4. *The Catholic Encyclopedia*, Vol. IX, New York: Robert Appleton, 1910. See: newadvent.org/cathen/09152a.htm.
5. Philias F. Bourgeois, *Vie de l'abbé François-Xavier Lafrance*, Montreal: Librairie Beauchemin, 1913, p. 95.
6. Quoted by Denise Rodrigue, *Le Cycle de Pâques au Québec et dans l'ouest de la France*, Quebec: Presses de l'Université Laval, 1983, p. 188.

*Le Moniteur acadien* reminded its readers of the compulsory Lenten regulations:

> By virtue of an indult, except for Palm Sunday, the use of meat is permitted on Sundays and also on the Monday, Tuesday and Thursday of the first five full weeks; but on those days, people required to fast may only eat meat at one meal. Likewise, on the days when meat is allowed, it is forbidden to use fish or oysters and meat at the same meal.
>
> By virtue of the same indult, when preparing dishes with meat it is permitted to substitute fat or lard for butter or oil. This permission applies to all the fasting days of the year, but does not include that of having soup made with meat.
>
> Without breaking the fast in the morning, it is permitted to eat about two ounces of bread with a small quantity of a beverage of some kind, and about eight ounces for the evening collation.
>
> A grave offence is committed every time one disregards the obligation to fast, without sufficient reason, or if in doubt, without its being deemed permissible by one's priest or spiritual advisor.[7]

Throughout the twentieth century, Lenten regulations continued to be softened. In 1949, for example, the Church no longer prescribed fasting except on Ash Wednesday and Good Friday. After the Second Vatican Ecumenical Council in 1966, the Canadian bishops rescinded all regulations regarding not only the obligation to fast during Lent but also the obligation to abstain from eating meat on Fridays. They declared that the faithful were now free to practise the penance of their choice.

Lent was not just a time for fasting and abstaining from meat. Even after the obligation to fast was mitigated in 1949, people refrained from eating pastries and sweets during the weeks of spiritual preparation for the celebration of the resur-

---

7. "Le Mercredi des Cendres," *Le Moniteur acadien*, 6 February 1894, p. 2. The article in question was taken from the *Semaine religieuse*.

rection of Christ. It was also customary to refrain from any form of amusement. No weddings took place during Lent; there were no evenings of music and dance; young men could not go to visit their girlfriends; and many people even gave up playing cards. The Church asked the faithful to devote more time to prayer and, if possible, to attend more frequently the religious services in their parish church. The clergy encouraged parishioners to relive the Passion of Christ by making the Stations of the Cross regularly, if not daily, either at church or at home. As the correspondent for the newspaper *L'Évangéline* living in West Pubnico, Nova Scotia, indicated in 1935, the daily routine changed abruptly after the festivities of Mardi Gras: "We set aside games and pleasures and began a period of penance. On Wednesday, there was a large attendance for the morning mass and for the Way of the Cross in the evening, and many people received ashes. Every Wednesday and Friday evening during Lent, we have the Way of the Cross and the Benediction of the Blessed Sacrament."[8]

A few weeks later, a correspondent from Acadieville, New Brunswick, sent similar information, proof that life varied little from one Acadian village to another: "We have Lenten services every evening in the sacristy, and we also have the Way of the Cross on Wednesday and Friday evenings that we all make our duty to attend."[9] Several years earlier, in 1922, another New Brunswick correspondent, this time from Cocagne, noted the arrival of Lent by pointing out the beneficial effects of penances such as abstaining from smoking:

> Cigarettes are less stylish during the holy forty days. So much the better! I think Lent for some people should be continuous, and even then they would allow themselves on occasion to disregard the laws of abstinence. Let us hope that these cigarette smokers will not resume their old habit

8. *L'Évangéline*, 14 March 1935, p. 5.
9. *L'Évangéline*, 28 March 1935, p. 4.

> which is so harmful first of all to their financial situation and secondly to their health, as competent doctors attest.[10]

Giving up smoking for Lent was a popular penance among men, as was abstention from alcohol. However, it was customary for people of all ages to make their own personal Lenten resolutions.

10. *L'Évangéline*, 23 March 1922, p. 5.

# The Origins of Mi-Carême

As a rule, the demands of Lent were respected by Catholics, although this period of penance that began on Ash Wednesday and ended on Holy Saturday seemed like an eternity for young people. As was mentioned previously, the Catholic Church had gradually softened its Lenten restrictions so that by the end of the nineteenth century, Sundays had become days of grace when most people took a break from their penances. Young men went to see their girlfriends, family cooks took advantage of the opportunity to serve a dessert, and enthusiastic card players enjoyed a few games with friends or relatives.

Mi-Carême, however, offered the most anticipated and appreciated break in the Lenten period. It gave people the chance to really enjoy themselves again for a day, and even longer in some communities.

Although the middle of Lent falls on the fourth Thursday after Mardi Gras, the origins of Mi-Carême remain unknown. According to some historians, it developed during the seventh or eighth century. At some point, the actual day of Mid-Lent was shifted from the fourth Thursday to the fourth Sunday in Lent, known as Laetare Sunday — so called because the first word of the mass is "Laetare," which means "Rejoice" in Latin. The liturgy of this fourth Sunday is characterized by a joyful spirit that contrasts with all the other more sombre and austere Sundays of Lent.[11] It would appear, however, that many Catholics, notably in France, continued celebrating

---

11. *The Catholic Encyclopedia, op. cit.* See: newadvent.org/cathen/09152a.htm.

Mi-Carême on the Thursday, a tradition that eventually crossed the Atlantic Ocean and was preserved by the Acadians. Until the mid-1960s, Mi-Carême remained a special day for Acadians because their daily life was still punctuated by the rituals of the Catholic religion and because Lenten privations were still practised. Although it was not officially sanctioned by the Church, people took a breather from their penances to rekindle the joie-de-vivre in their community. Above all, Mi-Carême was a time for masks and welcoming mummers or masqueraders, known as Mi-Carêmes.

If the traditions associated with Mi-Carême arrived in Acadie in the seventeenth or early eighteenth century, they came discreetly without leaving any evidence in the documents of the time. At least, historians have not yet uncovered any written traces of Mi-Carême celebrations. This is not surprising since documents dating from that period were written, for the most part, by administrators or members of the clergy who rarely described the daily lives of ordinary people. Customs related to popular festivities were hardly ever mentioned, even with regard to Christmas.[12]

The oldest reference to the celebration of Mi-Carême by Acadians only dates back to 1878. That year in Miscouche, Prince Edward Island, the nun responsible for the annals of Saint Joseph's Convent run by the Congrégation de Notre-Dame wrote a few words that we can truly appreciate today. She made a point of noting that Mi-Carême, like Mardi Gras, was celebrated in this little Acadian village and that the convent school respected these local traditions. On Mardi Gras (Shrove Tuesday), the nun simply wrote in the diary of the convent: "Full holiday." In the case of Mi-Carême, which came several weeks later, she noted in her beautiful handwriting: "Another

---

12. Georges Arsenault, *Acadian Christmas Traditions*, Charlottetown: Acorn Press, 2007, pp. 18–19.

full holiday; in the evening the children received a number of visitors for the occasion."[13]

Several years later, the celebrations for Mi-Carême were also mentioned in a document written by a religious official located a long way from Prince Edward Island. An ordinance forbidding certain customs was published by Monsignor François-Xavier Bossé, the first Apostolic Prefect of the Gulf of St. Lawrence, who served the villages on the North Shore of Quebec, inhabited mainly by Acadian families from the Magdalen Islands and the Gaspé Peninsula. This ordinance, dated 25 January 1885, stipulates that a severe punishment would be reserved for people who play "tricks" on the eve of All Saints' Day (Halloween) or who, at any time of the year, "disguise themselves and wear a mask to go running around the roads making house-visits, as is done on Mardi Gras and Mi-Carême, and also for people who encourage them, let them in their house or other buildings, or let their children or servants do it."[14] The prefect was obviously not planning to go lightly on people who disobeyed his ordinance. First of all, they would be excluded from receiving the sacraments for one year and would not be eligible as godparents during this period. In addition, if they died without making amends, the guilty individuals would be buried "privately" in the parish cemetery without the customary prayers and funeral ceremonies which would not take place until the period of punishment had ended. And what would Msgr. Bossé do if the sinners were children or young people who had not yet made their First Communion? They would be prohibited from hearing mass for six months. In order to ensure that parents took their children's misdemeanour seriously, he declared that "parents are required to detain their children as soon as they are certain of their guilt, otherwise they are committing a grievous sin."

---

13. Annals of St. Joseph's Convent of the Congrégation de Notre-Dame in Miscouche. The convent school, also a boarding school, opened in 1864.

14. *Mandement des évêques du golfe St-Laurent*, Vol. I (1668–1905), Hauterive: Chancellerie de l'évêché, 1960, p. 113.

This order was to be read on the Sunday before Mardi Gras and before All Saints' Day. Needless to day, Msgr. Bossé's ordinance was not popular and certainly did not contribute to elevating him in the esteem of his flock. Placide Vigneau (1842–1926), a local chronicler and one of the founders of Pointe-aux-Esquimaux (today called Havre-Saint-Pierre), was very critical of the Apostolic Prefect: "Perhaps it might be a bit rash to say that Msgr. Bossé despised us; he certainly seemed to have a very low opinion of us, and any time he had the opportunity to humiliate us for whatever reason, he would seize the occasion whole-heartedly. Anyone who was alive when he was staying in Pointe-aux-Esquimaux would remember that."[15] According to Placide Vigneau, the famous order was read by the parish priest, Pierre Théberge, every year until he left the village in 1894, but the order "did not outlast him."[16]

Fortunately, not all members of the Catholic clergy manifested that kind of hostility towards customs such as the Mi-Carême celebrations. Father Philias F. Bourgeois (1855–1913), the first true Acadian ethnologist, was certainly very open-minded.[17] In 1888, when he was serving as parish priest in Havre Boucher in Antigonish County, Nova Scotia, he published an article in the newspaper *L'Évangéline* entitled "Mi-Carême and Our Customs of Bygone Days."[18] This well-written text (see page 27) is the oldest description of Acadian Mi-Carême traditions. He provides detailed first-hand obser-

15. Placide Vigneau, *Variétés de diverses farces et autres faits ridicules arrivés à la Pointe ou encore à des habitants de la Pointe*, original notes compiled by Guy Côté and Pierre Frenette in *Collection Nord-côtier*, No. 2, Société historique de la Côte-Nord, 1996, p. 60.

16. *Ibid.*, p. 63.

17. Ronald Labelle, "Philias-Frédéric Bourgeois : précurseur de l'ethnologie acadienne," *Francophonies d'Amérique*, No. 2, Presses de l'Université d'Ottawa, 1992, pp. 5–11.

18. "La Mi-Carême et nos coutumes d'autrefois," *L'Évangéline*, 7 March 1888, p. 2. The article was reprinted in the *Courrier des Provinces Maritimes*, 15 March 1888.

vations of the masked revellers or mummers who went visiting on Mi-Carême in Nova Scotia. He also mentions the mythical woman called the Mi-Carême who distributes sweets to well-behaved children — a character he probably encountered when he was growing up in the Memramcook Valley in New Brunswick.

Father Bourgeois felt that the celebration of Mi-Carême offered a necessary diversion for Acadian pioneers in a difficult period: "It was a physical need combined with a situational need arising from the painful tedium of their lonely forests and their condition as voluntary exiles in New France." The priest ethnologist was obviously pleased to report that the tradition was still alive amongst the Acadians: "In several localities in Nova Scotia, scenes from centuries past are replayed and reproduced with as much joy as in the days of our ancestors. It is surely a sign of the old French spirit that enjoys everything everywhere but needs distractions just the same."

In 1889, the year after Father Bourgeois published his article, another reference to Mi-Carême appeared in the newspaper *L'Évangéline*. The anonymous writer reported that a troupe of masqueraders or Mi-Carêmes went around Meteghan, in southwest Nova Scotia. Spreading good cheer throughout the parish, these joyful masked troubadours even stopped at the priest's house and the convent:

> Mi-Carême (or Demi-Carême) has arrived in the area. A troupe of individuals, dressed like old-fashioned bogeymen and escorted by a band of musicians with drums, fiddles, accordions and a host of other instruments, paid a call on the local elite, in particular our parish priest and Father Grace, who was here at the time. These masqueraders were greeted enthusiastically. They danced, jumped, and made a commotion in front of the two priests. The reverend gentlemen made a point of thanking this happy band for their visit. After offering greetings, songs, and traditional music, the members of the jubilant troupe made their way to the

convent where they repeated their performance for the pleasure of the sisters.[19]

Obviously feeling nostalgic, the correspondent from Meteghan gives the impression that this troupe had revived a tradition that had been abandoned in the village for some time: "They went around the neighbourhood. It was interesting and beautiful. It brought back memories of the good old days when everybody was close-knit, when everybody had fun together and helped each other out."

Articles of this kind published in Acadian newspapers are particularly valuable since they offer contemporaneous descriptions of the Mi-Carême tradition as it was practised in the 1880s in certain areas of Nova Scotia, the cradle of old Acadie. However, to really appreciate the undeniable wealth of Acadian Mi-Carême traditions, one is forced to turn to testimonies gathered since the middle of the twentieth century by folklorists, ethnologists, and students enrolled in classes on Acadian folklore at the Université de Moncton or the Université Sainte-Anne. These testimonies, given by people born after the 1870s, take us not only to Acadian hamlets and villages scattered throughout the Maritime provinces but also to several Acadian regions in Quebec, most notably the Gaspé Peninsula, the North Shore, and the Magdalen Islands.

The innumerable memories of Mi-Carême, collected from Acadians over a wide geographical area, show both the evolution and the diversity of the tradition. In most regions, Mi-Carême was celebrated by going around visiting or "running" in groups, but in some villages, the visiting was done by one person, called the Mi-Carême, who distributed candies to children. In a number of areas, the Mi-Carême was also an imaginary character who, at any time of the year, delivered babies or threatened naughty children.

---

19. *L'Évangéline*, 10 April 1889, p. 2.

## Mi-Carême and Our Customs of Bygone Days

Photo: Centre d'études acadiennes Collection

*The following article by Father Philias F. Bourgeois (1855–1913), published in the newspaper* L'Évangéline *on 7 March 1888, is the oldest known text on Acadian Mi-Carême celebrations. It was written when Father Bourgeois was serving as parish priest in Havre Boucher, in eastern Nova Scotia.*

The approach of Mi-Carême evokes disappearing customs and austerities rarely practised nowadays. Acadians in the olden days were strict Christians. For them, the holy quarantine meant a time of rigorous penance for which they carried out the regulations to the letter. The one exception was Mi-Carême or *Demi*-Carême, as they called it, using the long form still heard today. While remaining faithful to the essential obligations of the Lenten period, our forefathers took a few liberties on that day. They respected traditional holidays and *Demi*-Carême was one of them. Full of that joyful Gallic spirit that still characterizes them, they felt the need for distractions; it was a physical need combined with a situational need arising from the painful tedium of their lonely forests and their condition as voluntary exiles in New France. Consequently, young men and old men greeted the fourth Thursday of Lent with heartfelt joy. At nightfall, the young men would get together in various groups, and, equipped with outlandish costumes, masks, drums, bells, and old pots, they would choose their itinerary and decide on the program for their visits. After electing a leader, they would then set out. Whether they wanted to or not, they had to knock on every door. Not a single household could escape the antics of those happy lads, except for people who were still mourning a recent death.

There was great excitement everywhere, and everyone wanted to see the makeshift squad of *Demi*-Carême that was greeted with cheers everywhere. Carrying a defensive stick in one hand and musical instruments or noisemakers in the other, the unrecognizable visitors would make their solemn entrance into each house, and, after lining up in the modest living room, they would begin their concert. It would be pointless to describe the racket they made; suffice to say that their goal was to make a deafening noise and above all to play out of tune — the reward being delicious refreshments, prepared by the maid, which everyone attacked with a hearty appetite. After saying their good-byes, they would go off to entertain other neighbours.

Sometimes these squires of *Demi*-Carême made their entrance at the very moment when the members of a family were gathered together in the presence of the Lord, piously reciting the rosary. Thereupon, our visitors would kneel down immediately and respond respectfully to the prayer. Sometimes after a decade, when the head of the family was saying the *Gloria Patri* and everyone had their heads bowed, a knight wearing a visor would ring the bell more or less irreverently. But a severe glance directed at the blasphemous individual called him to order and the rosary was completed in earnest. After the prayers were over, the adventurous group would stand up noisily. Seated in his old wooden armchair, the master of the house would sing the traditional song of *Demi*-Carême and then the dancing would begin. Terrified by the indescribable leaping about, the old woman of the house would huddle in a corner, numerous chairs would be knocked over, the young children would be roaring with laughter, and, in the midst of all this hullabaloo, the tireless prowlers of *Demi*-Carême would disappear, after having said their good-byes to the whole family. In some parts of Nova Scotia, these scenes from centuries past were repeated with as much joy as in the days of our ancestors. That indeed is the old French spirit that takes pleasure in everything everywhere but needs distractions just the same. Peasants in Burgundy still observe these festivities on the first Sunday of Lent. They eat *galotte* [pancakes] and *garguche* [doughnuts], make bonfires that light up public places, perform round dances, and the next day they go back to their Lenten penance with more devotion than ever.

In New Brunswick, at least in some of the French areas, these diversions take place nowadays on Mardi Gras, the eve of Lent. However, the Mi-Carême also contributed her share of legends. She is similar to the English Santa Claus. A woman said to be as old as the Wandering Jew symbolizes Mid-Lent. In the middle of the forty days, she goes from house to house enquiring about the children's behaviour. She distributes rewards to obedient children, but punishes naughty children and sometimes even takes away the incorrigible ones. Imagine the terror that reigns among children during those eight days! At the time of the Crusades, it would appear that by merely pronouncing the name of Richard the Lion Heart, Moslem mothers could make their children tremble. Even today, our good Acadian mothers can still do the same thing by threatening their untamable offspring with the wrath of the Mi-Carême.

However, these festivities and superstitious stories are no longer as fashionable as they used to be, nor is the old Acadian faith as strong. One is not necessarily dependent on the other, but I think they are linked to each other in a tangible manner. A famous writer of this century uttered a truth which, by way of comparison, is very applicable in this case: "Some people are surprised that society is becoming sad, that it is becoming sombre, and that it no longer laughs with the healthy laughter of the olden days. It seems to me that this change is easy to explain: when the waves of a river have no defined shores to contain them, the river will overflow on all sides and have no depth anywhere. The same is true of pleasure: when it is spread out evenly every day, when it has no boundaries or hindrances, it no longer has any intensity; it barely causes people to smile, like the guest who comes visiting too often..." That certainly explains those joyous ceremonies of the past, that gentle outpouring on certain days when all the neighbours gathered together in a communion of thoughts and feelings, cementing unity and peace in every rank of society, when people's faces expressed joy and serenity because their hearts were once laden with pain and misery. Indeed, the myths of terror and joyful distractions of Mi-Carême hardly exist anymore. Our culture denigrates them, perhaps rightfully so. Our culture pushes them away, but is it not pushing away something else? Customs can change with the centuries, but faith does not change. Any change is a loss that leads quickly to indifference and eventually to renunciation.

On the day after *Demi*-Carême, our forefathers resumed their strict regime of penance. They knew how to enjoy themselves by combining their rejoicings with the celebration of their religious feasts, but they also knew how to believe, obey, suffer, hope, and pray. Despite these momentary diversions, the Lenten rule was a sacred law they observed faithfully and, in that, we should be like them. They did not seek compromises with heaven. If, for a moment, they stepped into pleasure, they did not step aside when there was a sacrifice to be made. They knew how to pick up their cross and carry it, whereas we barely know how to drag it without picking it up...

# The Mythical Woman Called the Mi-Carême

Alice Richard's family in Saint-Philippe, Prince Edward Island, called the mysterious woman who visited her home at dusk handing out candies to the little children the "*Grande* Mi-Carême." The addition of the adjective for "big" helped distinguish this solitary individual from the other masked people (called Mi-Carêmes) who went around the neighbourhood in small groups on the same evening. The "big" Mi-Carême that Alice Richard saw in the 1940s always walked with a cane and was just disguised with a white sheet that went from head to toe.[20]

This mysterious woman is far from having been an isolated family custom. She frequented most of the Acadian villages in Prince Edward Island where she still makes her annual visits in the West Prince area. She also used to be seen in southwest New Brunswick and in at least one Nova Scotian community.

Father Philias F. Bourgeois wrote briefly about the woman known as the Mi-Carême in his article published in 1888. He compares her to the myth of Santa Claus:

> She is similar to the English Santa Claus. A woman said to be as old as the Wandering Jew symbolizes Mid-Lent. In the middle of the forty days, she goes from house to house enquiring about the children's behaviour. She distributes rewards to obedient children, but punishes naughty children and sometimes even takes away the incorrigible ones.[21]

---

20. Alice (Bernard) Richard, *La petite histoire de Papa*, self-published, [1977], p. 51.
21. Bourgeois, *loc. cit.*

This Mi-Carême obviously originates in France where she was known in the northwestern part of the country. In Normandy, for example, children used to put their shoes beside the fireplace so that during the night "Mother" Mi-Carême, as she was referred to, would bring them presents which usually consisted of a cone filled with prunes or other dried fruit. As a warning for naughty children, she would leave switches.[22] According to the folklorist Paul-Yves Sébillot, there was also an imaginary woman in Brittany who, like Santa Claus, travelled through the skies: "In Brittany she appeared on the day in the unexpected form of a beautiful lady, called Madam Mi-Carême, who rode across the sky on horseback shaking treats from her golden horn for children who had been taken to wayside crosses to see her go by. Needless to say, they never saw her, but candies seemed to fall from the sky."[23] Little children in Brittany would thank Madam Mi-Carême by leaving a bit of hay for her horse at the foot of the village cross. In Upper Britanny, children were told to take a little bundle of hay into the garden for the Mi-Carême who, in exchange, would leave candies and toys for them in the box trees or the laurels.[24]

A few references to this personified form of the feast day have also been found in Quebec, the oldest of which appears in *Charles Guérin*, a novel by Pierre-Joseph-Olivier Chauveau (1820–1890) published in 1852. During an evening party on Mi-Carême held in a rich farmer's home, the Mi-Carême arrives disguised as an "old woman who was literally bent double and whose face we finally discovered at the bottom of an old funnel-shaped hat [...] She supported herself with a large hooked

---

22. René Stibel, "Coutume de Mi-Carême en Normandie," *La Tradition*, Vol. VI, 1892, p. 135 quoted by Anne-Marie Desdouits in *La vie traditionnelle au pays de Caux et au Canada français. Le cycle des saisons*, Quebec: Presses de l'Université Laval, 1987, p. 175.

23. Paul-Yves Sébillot, *Le Folklore de la Bretagne*, Paris: G.-P. Maisonneuve & Larose, 1968, p. 312.

24. Arnold Van Gennep, *Manuel de Folklore français contemporain*, Tome I, Vol. 3, Paris: A. & J. Picard, 1947, p. 989.

## Here and There According to Sylvain

Here comes the Mi-Carême. Did the Mi-Carême ever give you presents? I remember seeing her several times when I was a child. She gave me a big sugar loaf once and warned me that it would change into soap if I was naughty. That kind lady spoke from under her big blanket in a tone of voice that strangely resembled my Aunt Marguerite's. When she stretched out her arm to hand me her precious gift, my suspicions were confirmed at the sight of my Aunt's very familiar hand, especially her silver ring that she was so proud of and that my Uncle Laurent had brought her from the city a long time ago. Alas, these old customs of ours are disappearing too quickly. Because of the demands of modern life, we no longer have the leisure to keep up these lovely legends from the "good old days." Our children are becoming more and more precocious. The poetry and harmless illusions of the young are giving way to the rough prose and realism of the twentieth century. Perhaps we are better off; we will let the ethnologists discuss the matter, but we all watch with regret as our cherished ways and customs disappear.

By Sylvain

Source: *L'Impartial* (Tignish, Prince Edward Island)
14 March 1907

stick and was carrying a huge sack on her back."[25] Her face was blackened, she was wearing glasses without lenses, and she was dressed in rags "from which hung fish tails and fish bones." Like the Acadian Mi-Carême, she brought sweets for obedient children: "To the children who had stayed up especially for this visitor who they had been anxiously awaiting for several weeks, she gave different presents, depending on their behaviour. The ones who had been good received sugar-coated nuts or some sugar and those who had been bad got frozen potatoes or nut shells carefully wrapped in paper..."

Chauveau was probably describing a custom in his native village of Charlesbourg, near Quebec City. In 1887, Father Charles Trudelle, from the same village, published the history of his native parish in which he also mentions the legendary woman: "Every year at nightfall on Mi-Carême, we witnessed the arrival of the mysterious old wife of Pierre Beaulieu who was told ahead of time by our dear mothers about our little pranks and acts of mischief and for which she took us to task saying that it was her little finger who had told her everything. We made lots of nice promises to her, then she gave us some candies and said she'd be back next year."[26] It would appear that the tradition of the woman who handed out rewards on Mi-Carême disappeared in the province of Quebec before the end of the nineteenth century since there are no references indicating that she was still around in the twentieth.

As was the case in Charlesbourg, young Acadians usually had the opportunity to see the Mi-Carême with their own eyes, and even to receive sweets directly from her hands. There were exceptions, however. Hermine Gaudet, who grew up in Egmont Bay, Prince Edward Island, in the 1910s, remembers

---

25. Quoted by E.-Z. Massicotte in "La Mi-Carême," *Bulletin des recherches historiques*, Vol. XXXII, 1926, pp. 136–9.

26. Charles Trudelle, *Paroisse de Charlesbourg*, Québec: Imprimerie Générale A. Côté, 1887, pp. x–xi.

that the Mi-Carême would come to her house while she was in school. When she got home, her mother would say to her, "I think the Mi-Carême was here." In accordance with the tradition, the visitor left gifts on the wood pile.[27] In Lauraine Léger's home in Saint-Paul-de-Kent, New Brunswick, in the 1930s, the Mi-Carême made her annual rounds, but nobody ever saw her either:

> At our place, we'd put out our cap (a kind of tuque we wore in the winter) behind the house. We lined up our caps because we were told that the Mi-Carême would come and put some candies in them. We'd go back inside the house. An hour and a half later, my mother would say: "Well, perhaps you can go out now and see if the Mi-Carême has been by." And, sure enough, we went out and there would be three, four, or five candies in each cap. Then we'd come back into the house as happy as anything.[28]

Lauraine Léger remembers that her mother warned her children not to go out too soon because you were not supposed to see the Mi-Carême. Even if children never caught sight of her, they had an idea what this invisible visitor looked like: "People said she wore some kind of long coat or cape. Some people also said she had a big bag for taking away the children who'd been bad. Oh! That really scared us a lot."

The most notable characteristic of the Mi-Carême was usually her threatening demeanour. She was supposed to frighten children, as Lydia LeBlanc from Rogersville, New Brunswick, relates:

> I frightened kids more than once. You'd dress completely in white, with a big white sheet. You'd wrap it around your body and then put on gumshoes. To be scary, you'd shake your arms. Kids thought you were going to grab them. I made house-visits myself disguised as the Mi-Carême and

27. Georges Arsenault Collection, Recording 1554.

28. Georges Arsenault Collection.

> I did frighten my own kids. I had a stick for banging on the floor.[29]

Some children seem to have been traumatized when the Mi-Carême was overly aggressive. This was the case for François Robichaud from Pointe-Sapin, New Brunswick, who told the folklorist Sister Catherine Jolicoeur that the only thing in his life that ever scared him was the Mi-Carême:

> We were so scared of her. Well me, I could have died. She'd stuff us into a bag to frighten us. If you hadn't listened, she'd put you in a bag. Oh, yes! Then we'd hide, my goodness! I saw her putting little kids in that bag, then [pretending] to take them away. They practically died! Nowadays, they wouldn't let you do that, because it could harm a child for life, you see?[30]

All children were not traumatized to this extent, because deep down most of them knew that it was just a game, even if they were terrified at the time. Marcella Perry of Tignish, Prince Edward Island, has fond memories of the Mi-Carême who came to her house in the 1950s and 1960s. In those days, she did not realize that it was one of her older sisters who was wearing the mask: "She scared us, so we hid behind my mother. She wanted us to go get the treat she'd brought us. But she frightened us so much that we didn't want to go and get it, so she'd tease us just to see how brave we were."[31] As Marcella Perry explains, her mother always made a point of being around when the Mi-Carême came visiting in order to reassure or comfort the little ones if need be:

> I know that one of my sisters, who was about three years old, was crying and crying. The more she cried, the more the Mi-Carême screamed. That made for a lot of noise in the

29. CEA, Catherine Jolicoeur Collection, Recording 13,678. Mrs. LeBlanc was 85 years old in 1977.
30. CEA, Catherine Jolicoeur Collection, Recording 11,845. Mr. Robichaud was 85 years old in 1977.
31. Georges Arsenault Collection.

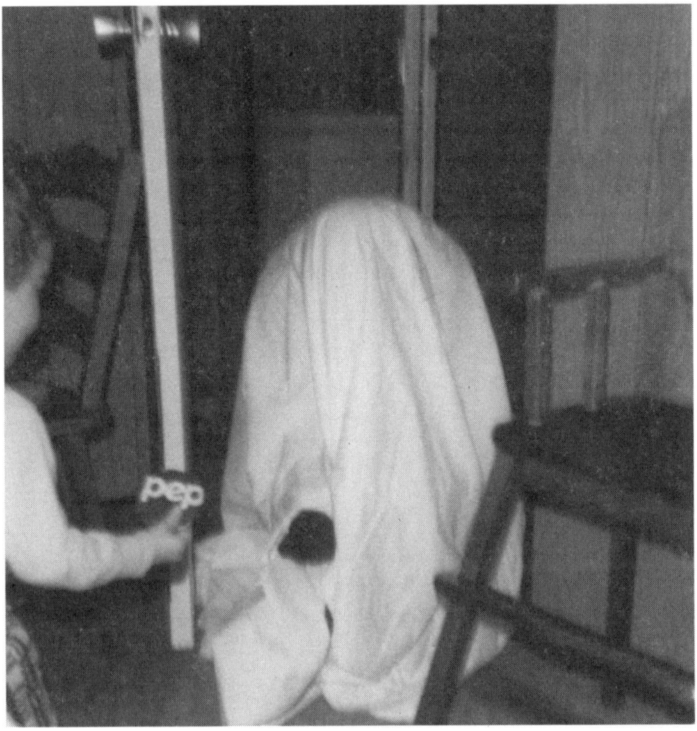


**The Mi-Carême with a black hand.** David Deveaux, Rita Poirier's nephew, has just been given a chocolate bar by the Mi-Carême on the occasion of her visit in 1982. According to the tradition in the Poirier family of St. Edward, Prince Edward Island, the Mi-Carême always wears a sheet or a blanket and has black hands. (Ellen Deveaux Collection)

> kitchen! I remember we'd start to come out from behind my mother to get closer to the Mi-Carême, then she'd let out a screech and bang her stick. Then we'd go back behind [my mother] again. The Mi-Carême kept teasing us. She never hit us with her stick though. But she came pretty close to it sometimes.

After the visitor had gone, Mrs. Perry tried to make her brood understand that the Mi-Carême was not as mean as she seemed: "She's not here to hurt you. She's here to give you candies. Don't be afraid of the Mi-Carême." Trusting their mother implicitly, the children said to themselves, "Well, if Mom says so, it's okay." Otherwise, according to Marcella, "she'd have had babies crying all night long!"

The Mi-Carême's most common disguise was simply a blanket or a white sheet that covered her completely. To prevent her legs from showing, she would walk all bent over so the blanket almost touched the ground. Since there were no holes cut out for her eyes, the Mi-Carême's field of vision was greatly reduced. Consequently, she moved around very little and was content to stay close to the door if she went into the house. The Mi-Carême made sure not to use a blanket that the children she was visiting would recognize, such as a distinctive quilt that they might have noticed on a bed somewhere in the neighbourhood. As a result, the Mi-Carême tended to be prudent and usually just wore a plain white sheet. Sometimes, without thinking, she would grab the first blanket she could put her hands on. Arthur Thibodeau, from St. Edward, Prince Edward Island, recalls that one year the Mi-Carême smelled really bad. She had put on her disguise in the stable, using a horse blanket probably without imagining the consequences! Detecting the odour immediately, the little ones exclaimed without any inhibition, "The Mi-Carême smells bad tonight. She stinks tonight!"[32]

Rita Poirier's mother, also from St. Edward, said that the Mi-Carême hid under a blanket because she was too ugly to show her face. Her hands were always black. In any case, that was the only part of her body the children saw when they went close to her to receive their gifts.[33] They could also catch a glimpse of what she was wearing on her feet, usually big rubber boots which the shrewder children were sometimes able to recognize.

From time to time, the mysterious stranger would forego the blanket in favour of a somewhat more sophisticated dis-

32. Georges Arsenault Collection.

33. Georges Arsenault Collection.

guise. Evelyn Arsenault recalls that at her home in Nail Pond, Prince Edward Island, the Mi-Carême "was decked out like an old grandmother."[34] Her costume included a long dress, an old hat pulled down over her head with a kerchief that also served to cover part of her face. A pair of old-fashioned glasses completed her disguise. "We didn't recognize her with her old glasses," Mrs. Arsenault recalled.

Sometimes the Mi-Carême took on the appearance of a man. Such was the case at Lorette Arsenault's in Saint-Joseph in the Memramcook Valley in New Brunswick, where a rather elderly woman from the neighbourhood made the rounds every year at Mi-Carême, with her face blackened and wearing a man's cap. On some occasions, it was hard to determine the sex of the Mi-Carême, as Eugène Perry from Tignish explains: "I was the Mi-Carême. I put a big cushion on my back, then we found the biggest jacket we could find, then a long dress. Oh! That scared the devil!"[35]

After the Mi-Carême left the house, parents made sure their children did not see in which direction she went. Some parents did not even want their little ones to see her feet, for fear they would recognize her boots. Rita Perry, also from Tignish, says that people believed that it would bring bad luck if you saw which way the Mi-Carême went because she might not come back the next year. Consequently, when the Mi-Carême was getting ready to leave the house, the children had to bow their heads and look down at the floor. One year, it appears that several children said they saw the Mi-Carême's feet and noticed that they were very large![36] Others supposedly found one of her shoes which had the following inscription inside: "Marguerite, daughter of Jean Djullant, heel on back to front."[37]

34. Georges Arsenault Collection.

35. Georges Arsenault Collection, Recording 1274.

36. Georges Arsenault Collection, ms. 123.

37. Georges Arsenault Collection, Recording 811. Informant: Obéline DesRoches, born in 1872 in Urbainville, PEI.

## Hello Mi-Carême

*The following story was told to Sister Catherine Jolicoeur in 1976 by Mrs. Élise Brun (1899–1997) from Cap-Pelé, New Brunswick. Her grandparents lived in Grand-Digue.*

On Mi-Carême, we'd go to Grandmother's house. She'd say, "It's Mi-Carême today. You gotta be nice all day. When the Mi-Carême comes, I'll let you know."

When the Mi-Carême arrived, Grandmother would say, "Look out the window." We'd look out the window and see the Mi-Carême in the apple orchard. She had a big white sheet over her head. We couldn't see that Grandfather was underneath it. Grandmother would say, "Go on out and say 'Hello Mi-Carême.'" So we'd go and say, 'Hello Mi-Carême.' He'd stretch his hand out from under the sheet and give us each a cookie made of dough shaped like a little man. It was baked with fir needles on top. Grandmother said, "You gotta say 'Thank you Mi-Carême,' then you gotta eat them."

We'd go back home, then we'd eat them. They were really awful. They tasted like fir needles, but we'd eat them any way. Grandmother said we had to eat them. If we didn't eat them, the Mi-Carême might take us off into the woods. We were really scared. Oh, we were sure scared of the Mi-Carême. Grandmother said that the Mi-Carême lived in the woods: "You can tell she lives in the woods because when she made those cookies, I think it was under a fir tree and the needles were falling off."

Source: Centre d'études acadiennes,
Catherine Jolicoeur Collection, Recording 7882.

*Illustration: Denise Paquette*

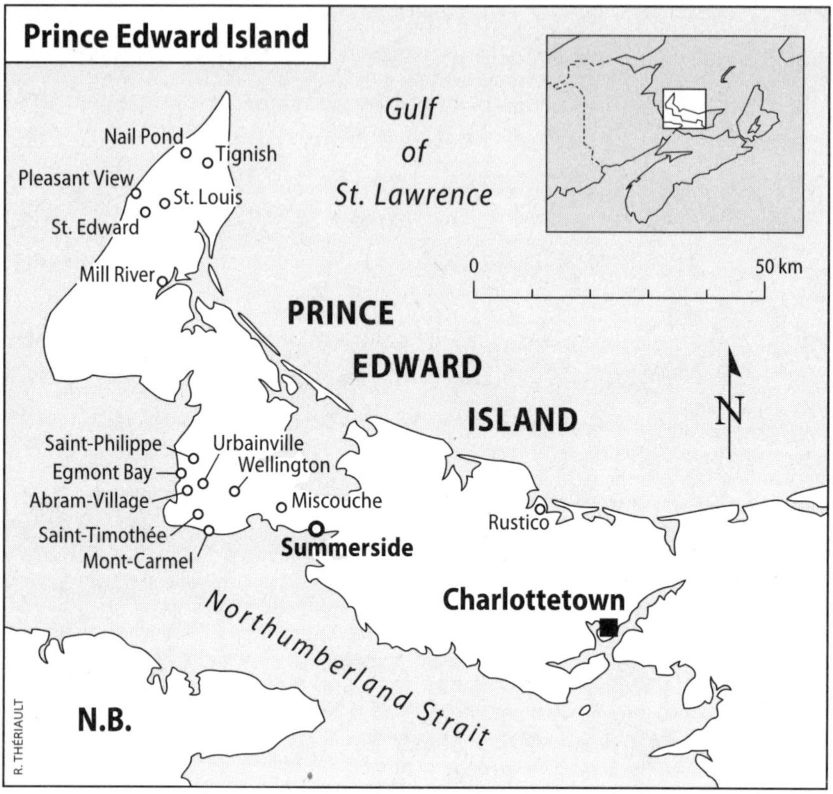


There was never any secret as to where the Mi-Carême came from: everybody knew for a fact that she lived in the woods. As the fourth Thursday of Lent approached, many little children would cast nervous glances in the direction of the wood lots, thinking perhaps that they might see the Mi-Carême's shadow. And just so there would be no doubt in their minds as to where she came from, the cookies she brought often contained needles from a coniferous tree! As Alyre Landry, from Notre-Dame, New Brunswick, recalls, "The Mi-Carême lived back in the woods, and to prove that she lived in the woods, she made cookies with needles in them."[38] He also says the woman from the woods used to throw biscuits at them: "I got one right in my forehead!"

38. CEA, Catherine Jolicoeur, Recording 10,419.

In one family in Mont-Carmel, Prince Edward Island, the Mi-Carême's cookies did not have any strange ingredients, but they were enormous, measuring about fifteen centimetres (six inches) in diameter. That proved to the children that the cookies were not made by their mother, but by the mysterious woman.[39] In addition to cookies, the Mi-Carême might also bring fudge, store-bought candies, or even apples. As a general rule, she handed out these treats parsimoniously since, as everyone knew, she led a meagre existence in the woods. She could not afford any extravagances, especially since, in those days, Acadian villages had a lot of young children. In one family alone, there might be up to six little ones awaiting her visit. A child would feel very privileged if he or she was lucky enough, in the middle of Lent, to get one or two cookies, a big piece of fudge, a little taffy, a few candies, or even just an apple.

Like Santa Claus, the Mi-Carême was not supposed to reward badly behaved children. Parents took it upon themselves to remind their children that if they were disobedient, the Mi-Carême would not bring them any treats, or, worse still, she would pick them up and take them off to the woods! Numerous testimonies indicate that the Mi-Carême rarely carried out the parents' threats! Only one person informed us that the Mi-Carême left herring tails when she was visiting Urbainville, Prince Edward Island. At the age of 101, Obéline DesRoches still remembered the occasion: "She gave us that once at our place, along with raw potatoes. She played that trick on us once."[40] Based on the testimony of this venerable centenarian, it would seem that the Mi-Carême's gesture was designed more to tease than to punish.

Sometimes the Mi-Carême paid a visit to schoolchildren. When Éléonore DesRoches was teaching in the Tignish area of Prince Edward Island in the 1930s, she arranged for the

39. Georges Arsenault Collection, ms. 210.

40. CEA, Georges Arsenault Collection, Recording 811.

## I Had Some Terrible Scares

"Yes, I remember when we were young, there was a neighbour, an old woman. She'd put on a costume and bring us candies. I remember Mom would say, 'The Mi-Carême's going to come this afternoon, get ready.' She'd go out and put our caps on the woodpile. When the Mi-Carême came to the door, she'd jump up and down, and say, 'Cap, cap!' Then we'd all look out the window. She'd come to put candies in our caps on the woodpile."

— **Lorette Arsenault** (Saint-Joseph de Memramcook, New Brunswick)

"On Mi-Carême, we got candies. Mom said it was the Mi-Carême who brought them. One year, I decided that I was going to try and see the Mi-Carême. To my surprise, I saw old Dina, wearing a big old black coat, heading towards our house. She gave candies to Mom and left. Later, Mom gave us some candies and said it was the Mi-Carême who brought them. But I knew better."

— **Gérard Boudreau** (Boudreau Office, New Brunswick)

"My father used to say, 'If you don't listen, the Mi-Carême won't come, she won't stop by.' In those days, people always did a wash on that day. When he'd come in from putting the clothes on the line, he'd say, 'Oh, I saw the Mi-Carême, she came by. Did you see her?' — No, I didn't. That's how he'd surprise us. He'd say, 'Go look outside. Go out behind the house.' And you'd find some candies that were hidden somewhere."

— **Melvin Gallant** (Saint-Timothée, Prince Edward Island)

"The earliest memories I have of the Mi-Carême are when she was played by Mrs. Annie, Alice's mother, Mrs. René Maddix. She'd come as soon as we got home from school, then she'd go around to all the houses. There were a lot of children in the houses in those days. She'd bring us sugar cookies with a raisin on top. I've never forgotten that. For many years when we arrived home from school, Mom would say to us, 'The Mi-Carême is going to drop by.' We'd watch for her. She had a big cane and she was disguised. She gave us cookies."

— **Roséline Gallant** (Egmont Bay, Prince Edward Island)

"There were some folks who got dressed up as old women, then they'd frighten the children. I had some terrible scares when I was little. My brother would get disguised secretly, then he'd frighten us. We always thought the Mi-Carême was someone who was going to take us away."

— **Théophile Blanchard** (Rustico, Prince Edward Island)

"That Mi-Carême would come across the fields. We'd wait for the Mi-Carême. We'd be watching everywhere: 'When's she coming?' The first thing we'd see was her coming across the fields with a big cane. She'd fall a couple of times; sometimes she'd be in the mud. She'd come to the door then she'd bang on the door. As soon as the children heard her they were so scared! She'd come in the house. She didn't talk. The Mi-Carême wasn't supposed to talk. She'd have her big cane, then she'd point at the floor to make the children dance. If the children danced, she'd give them a sucker or something. They were really scared of her, they'd move their feet around trying to dance. After they'd danced, they'd go hide in a corner. They were really frightened."

— **Evelyn Arsenault** (Tignish, Prince Edward Island)

Mi-Carême to come to her school with a basket of treats from the parents.[41] On occasion, the visitor would suddenly appear uninvited at the door of the little schoolhouse. This happened to Exélia Arsenault who was teaching in the same area between 1910 and 1920: "I was teaching in our district. Someone knocked on the door, dressed as a man. I couldn't tell if it was a man, well, it was dressed like the Mi-Carême. I was a bit uncomfortable because there were Protestants in the class and they didn't have the Mi-Carême. I let him in anyway. He made his rounds."[42]

Children in West Chezzetcook, Nova Scotia, also had the opportunity to see the Mi-Carême when they were in school. She was played by a spinster who lived in the neighbourhood. Year after year, she enjoyed disguising herself as the Mi-Carême, much to the pleasure of the pupils. She never actually went inside the school, but children like John Lapierre watched for her out the window: "She was dressed in white. She chose a spot where the children could see her. As soon as it was recess, out we went! We rushed out to see the Mi-Carême. She made little molasses cakes that she threw into the yard. The children went around picking them up."[43] You were not supposed to get too close to this Mi-Carême. Especially since she carried a stick to defend herself from the older pupils who might attempt to pull off her mask or mistreat her and, supposedly, she was also armed with a bag of pepper hidden under her sheet or perhaps even a big knife!

As one can see, it was not the duty of any specific person to play the role of the Mi-Carême. She was often a member of the family, either one of the grandparents, the father or the

41. CEA, Georges Arsenault Collection, Recording 781.

42. Centre de recherche acadien de l'Î.-P.-É., Société Saint-Thomas-Aquin fonds, Evéline Poirier Collection, Tape 9, Side B.

43. CEA, Ronald Labelle Collection, Recording 1384. See also: Ronald Labelle, *Acadian Life in Chezzetcook*, Lawrencetown Beach: Potterfield Press, 1995, pp. 48–50.

mother, an uncle or an aunt, or, in the case of large families, an older brother or sister. For instance, in Anne-Marie and Eugène Perry's home, in Tignish, Prince Edward Island, it was Eugène himself who dressed as the Mi-Carême for the firstborn children in his family of nine. Later he passed on the duty to Tish, one of his older daughters, when she was only a teenager. The Mi-Carême could also just be any man or woman who enjoyed playing the part and making the rounds of all his or her neighbours who had young children. Such was the case in Joan Fennessey's home in Tignish. The Mi-Carême she knew around 1950 visited several of the houses on her street but Joan was so terrified that her parents never let the visitor in. Nevertheless, the Mi-Carême left her a little bag of candies on the doorstep or in the tree beside the house.[44]

Many Irish families in Tignish and the neighbouring villages integrated the Acadian tradition of Mi-Carême into their own customs. Throughout the 1950s, in the hamlet called Christopher Cross inhabited for the most part by English-speaking Irish families, a Mi-Carême played by an Acadian woman paid a visit to the young Harpers, Handrahans, Hogans, and Readys.[45] Around the same time, the Mi-Carême in the fishing village of Miminegash visited the Irish families as well the Acadian families.[46] It is interesting to note that the term "mi-carême" is one of the rare French words that appears in T. K. Pratt's *Dictionary of Prince Edward Island English.* Pratt uses the anglicized spelling "mickram" and indicates that the term is well-known in the western part of the province[47] where intercultural marriages have been taking place over a long period and where the rate of anglicization of Acadians is now very high.

---

44. Georges Arsenault Collection, ms. 261.

45. Georges Arsenault Collection, ms. 266 and 267. Informants: Elizabeth Rankin (née Handrahan) and Joanne Arbing (née Handrahan).

46. Georges Arsenault Collection, ms. 263. Informant: Leo Butler.

47. T. K. Pratt, *Dictionary of Prince Edward Island English,* Toronto: University of Toronto Press, 1988, p. 97.

# A Lasting Custom

Throughout the twentieth century, the geographical territory frequented by the Mi-Carême, distributor of treats to little Acadians, gradually became smaller and smaller. In fact, it may have started shrinking in the previous century. Based on Annette LeBlanc's comments published in a parish monograph in 1986, this seems to have been the case in Sainte-Anne-de-Kent, New Brunswick. According to her, the tradition of the Mi-Carême was alive in the 1860s but it disappeared not long afterwards: "She came out of the woods, out of Odilon LeBlanc's cedar grove, wearing a costume and a mask and went around from house to house. People were frightened of her and would never have dared pull off her mask to see if they could recognize her."[48] In some villages in southeast New Brunswick, the Mi-Carême was still around in the 1930s and 1940s, and even a little later. Alméda Thibodeau remembers that when she was growing up in the village of Haute-Aboujagane in the 1950s, an eccentric woman, known as *la Vieille Dan* (Old Dan's Woman), used to disguise herself as the Mi-Carême and go around the neighbourhood: "She'd come around once a year, I'm sure she went to twenty or so houses close to where she lived. She'd walk from one house to the next, handing out candies and fudge."[49] In the case of Chezzetcook, Nova Scotia, the tradition of the Mi-Carême seems to have disappeared sometime during the early decades of the twentieth century.

It is hard to follow the comings and goings of the Mi-Carême, especially since she is so unobtrusive that she could easily visit

48. Father Anselme Chiasson and Arthur Poirier, *Sainte-Anne-de-Kent (1886–1986)*, Sainte-Anne-de-Kent: Les Éditions Chockpish, 1986, p. 119.

49. Georges Arsenault Collection.

two or three families in a village unbeknownst to anyone else in the community. That is what happens nowadays in the West Prince area of Prince Edward Island, the only Acadian region in the Maritimes where the Mi-Carême still brings treats to children. If you ask people in the area whether the Mi-Carême still makes her annual rounds, most of them would say that it has been a long time since she has been in their village. Although she goes to fewer homes than in the past, she has, in fact, never stopped making her house-visits. Perhaps she has just become more selective over the years.

According to a survey done in January 1980 of several Grade IV students at the elementary school in St. Louis, there were still many children in the villages of West Prince who knew about the Mi-Carême.[50] Lorie-Ann Perry, from Pleasant View, said that the Mi-Carême came to her house in 1979 around nine o'clock in the evening, dressed in black and wearing a cape, a veil, and boots. She even had false fingernails. Lorie-Ann said she was so frightened that she ran into her bedroom to hide but the Mi-Carême followed her and asked her in a low voice whether she had been a good girl. As a reward, the Mi-Carême gave her chocolates and chewing gum. That same year, Deborah Allain, another little girl from Pleasant View, also had a visit from the Mi-Carême. In addition to the black cape and the fake nails, she was wearing a red hat. Deborah said that her little sister was scared because the Mi-Carême had tried to put her in the bag she was carrying! The mysterious visitor, who in fact was their grandmother, proved to be very generous since she handed out candies and soap to the children and an oven mitt to their mother.

Most of the other pupils in the class who filled out the questionnaire had seen the Mi-Carême in the last few years. Arlene Laviolette, from St. Louis, said that the Mi-Carême came to her

50. The questionnaire on the Mi-Carême, developed by Georges Arsenault, was answered by ten children aged ten and eleven. See Georges Arsenault Collection, ms. 239–248.

home in 1978, covered in a blanket, wearing black boots and a hard hat, and carrying "a huge bag and a huge stick." When Arlene took part in the survey she knew that it was her father who had played the role of the Mi-Carême. In the final analysis, neither the appearance nor the habits of the Mi-Carême had changed much over the years. Her visits took place perhaps a little later in the evening than in the olden days and her gifts were more varied. In addition to candies, her treats included chewing gum, potato chips, and soft drinks which children really appreciated.

Since the 1980s, Alméda Thibodeau has contributed considerably to keeping the tradition of the mysterious Mi-Carême alive in West Prince, Prince Edward Island. When she moved from New Brunswick to St. Louis, her husband's native village, she decided to play the part of the Mi-Carême for her children and several of her little nieces and nephews who lived nearby. Alméda took her task seriously and made a point of getting to know the idiosyncrasies of the character according to the local customs: "She came from far away, she lived alone, she wasn't very sociable, she wasn't someone who talked a lot or stayed for a long time."[51] Alméda told the children what they should expect from this strange visitor: "She only comes because she likes children, but don't try and sit on her lap or anything like that, because she doesn't like it. But she likes you enough that she's going to bring you some candies because she knows what Lent's all about, then she's going to leave and go back to her place."

The threatening aspect of the Mi-Carême was the one characteristic that Alméda Thibodeau chose not to portray. She decided to play a Mi-Carême with a hideous face but an engaging personality. "At first," she said, "the children were a little bit frightened, but once they saw how things worked, they started to look forward to her, then they actually hugged

51. Georges Arsenault Collection.

**It's the Mi-Carême!** Joshua, Pamela, and Atlanta Perry, along with their grandmother, Marguerite Perry, greet the Mi-Carême as she enters their home in St. Louis, Prince Edward Island, around 1983. Would the children have realized that it was their mother, Alméda Thibodeau, hiding behind the mask? (Alméda Thibodeau Collection)

the Mi-Carême." In 1984, Alméda obtained a job with the Société Saint-Thomas-d'Aquin, the association for Acadians and Francophones in Prince Edward Island. Her cultural activity work led her to collaborate with the Club Ti-Pa, an Acadian social club in the West Prince area. Since the early 1980s, the club had been organizing an evening of entertainment for adults on Mi-Carême, which always included a visit from the mysterious woman associated with that time of year. Naturally, Alméda was invited several times to play the role. She even took part in the Radio-Canada morning show *Bonjour Atlantique* broadcast live on the occasion of the Mi-Carême celebrations, first in 1990 from the J.-Henri-Blanchard Centre, in Summerside, and then in 1992 from the Club Ti-Pa, in Tignish. Around the same time, she started getting dressed up as the Mi-Carême to

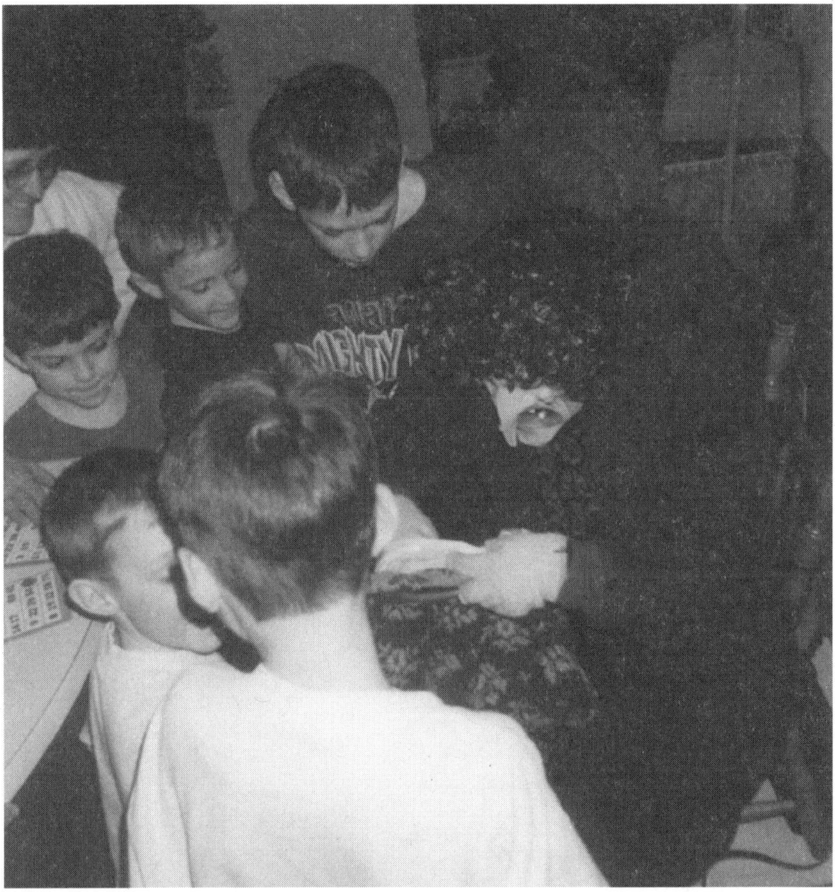

**What has she brought us?** The Mi-Carême (Alméda Thibodeau) visited Maurice and Kathleen Poirier's home in Mill River, Prince Edward Island, in 1994. Their children, and several nephews who had come over for the occasion, were anxious to see what the visitor had in her bag. (Maurice and Kathleen Poirier Collection)

go visiting elderly people in nursing homes. They were thrilled to welcome her and reminisce about their childhood and the days when they themselves had played the part of the Mi-Carême for their family.

Alméda Thibodeau went willingly to schools in her area to play the role of the Mi-Carême because she realized it was an excellent way to promote local Acadian traditions. Over the

**LA MI-CAREME PAYS VISIT**

DEBBIE HORNE/THE JOURNAL-PIONEER

**The students at St. Louis elementary school celebrated French Week with special lessons, projects and activities based on French Acadian heritage. During the celebrations the school had a visit from La Mi-Careme, a character from local folklore who came to the community every year mid-way into the Lenten season to treat the children with candy. Although she loved children, her appearance was sometimes quite frightful. However, the students here discovered La Mi-Careme was also a cheerful, funny character who was quite happy to share her treats with the entire student body. Walker Chaisson and Clancy Gilks had a chance to have a closer look at La Mi-Careme before she departed.**

*The Journal-Pioneer,* 19 March 2003.

years, she modified her woodland character so that schoolchildren would find her more interesting and informative. One year she arrived at the school sporting a long artificial nose. She told the children that it was to hide her real nose that Mimi, her pet squirrel, had chewed and disfigured. During subsequent visits

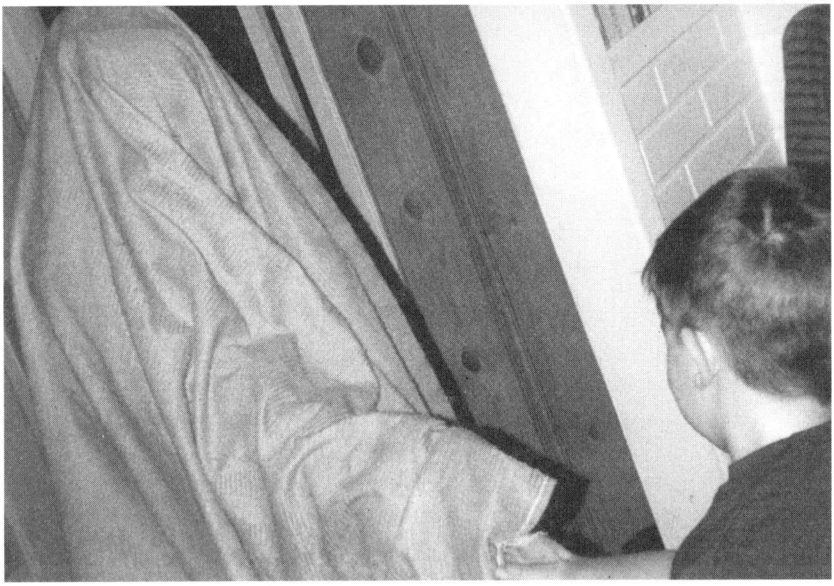

**Good evening Mi-Carême!** Little Logan Gallant bravely greets the Mi-Carême at the door of his home in St. Edward, Prince Edward Island, in 2000. (Edward and Fred Perry Collection)

in her role as the Mi-Carême, Alméda talked with the pupils about life in the woods with the wild animals and even brought a live squirrel with her to school. The teachers took the opportunity to do class projects in nature studies. As she says, her talks involved a certain amount of preparation: "I wasn't just going to put on a costume and go [to school] and come back home. I tried to plan my day." She obviously enjoyed meeting the schoolchildren and they were attached to her: "They all wanted to kiss me afterwards. All of them were happy and they talked about it for weeks."

The photograph of Alméda Thibodeau in her Mi-Carême costume appeared numerous times in both French- and English-language newspapers on the Island. The media coverage no doubt made people more aware of the legendary character associated with Mid-Lent and probably even motivated some Acadians to keep the tradition alive in their own families.

Edward and Freda Perry, from St. Edward, are Acadians who do not want to see the Mi-Carême disappear. As part of a cherished family tradition, they have always welcomed a visit from the Mi-Carême for their children and they do everything they can to make sure she does not forget the next generation. Like Alméda Thibodeau, the Perrys prefer not to use the mysterious woman as a way of threatening children. Nor do they limit her appearances to the fourth Thursday of Lent. She can make a surprise visit on any day during the winter, just wearing the traditional garb of a blanket. Edward and Freda Perry usually ask a neighbour to be the Mi-Carême since they like watching the children's reactions more than actually playing the role themselves.[52]

The Perrys think they are probably the only ones in their village who have preserved this ancient tradition. They point out that there are fewer and fewer children in St. Edward, as is the case everywhere else. Families of eight to fifteen children are a thing of the past and children no longer have to wait for a visit from the Mi-Carême to enjoy a few treats. They can have them every day, Lent or no Lent. As a result, the Mi-Carême no longer has the same appeal she used to have. Nevertheless, a number of people in this small Acadian region are anxious to continue transmitting the age-old tradition that they enjoyed so much in their own childhood. This is perhaps the main reason why the tradition of the Mi-Carême has survived. Brandon Chaisson, a fourteen-year-old boy from St. Edward, says that he hopes his children get to meet the Mi-Carême so they can have the same thrill he did when he was little, when she surprised him and frightened him and, of course, brought him a few goodies.

52. Georges Arsenault Collection.

# The Mi-Carême Will Come and Get You

Generally, the Mi-Carême was a character who frightened little children, whether it was the solitary character who handed out treats or any one of the individuals who went from house to house in a group. The image of the Mi-Carême often haunted little children for a long time before and after his or her brief visit to their homes in the middle of Lent. It is not surprising that parents added this legendary person to the list of other bogeymen such as the *Bonhomme Sept Heures*, the *Sournatchette,* or the *Marlèche*, whose names were used as threats to make children behave.[53] Writing about the Mi-Carême masqueraders on the Magdalen Islands, Father Anselme Chiasson states that, "In the past, their disguises and gesticulations easily took on a frightening appearance, so for the rest of the year naughty children were made to obey with the following threat: 'The Mi-Carême will come and get you!'"[54] According to Géraldine Chiasson, the same tactic was used in Lamèque, New Brunswick: "Children were often frightened of these strange and scary characters. So whenever they were bad, you just had to say to them, 'The Mi-Carême or the *Bonhomme Sept Heures* is going to come...' and the threat would have the desired effect."[55]

---

53. Regarding various bogeymen in French Canada, see *Héritage de la francophonie canadienne*, ed. Jean-Claude Dupont and Jacques Mathieu, Quebec: Les Presses de l'Université Laval, 1986, p. 88.

54. Father Anselme Chiasson, *Les îles de la Madeleine. Vie matérielle et sociale*, Montreal: Leméac, 1981, p. 151.

55. Géraldine Chiasson, *C'était la vie dans l'temps*, Tracadie (N.B.), 1990, p. 101.

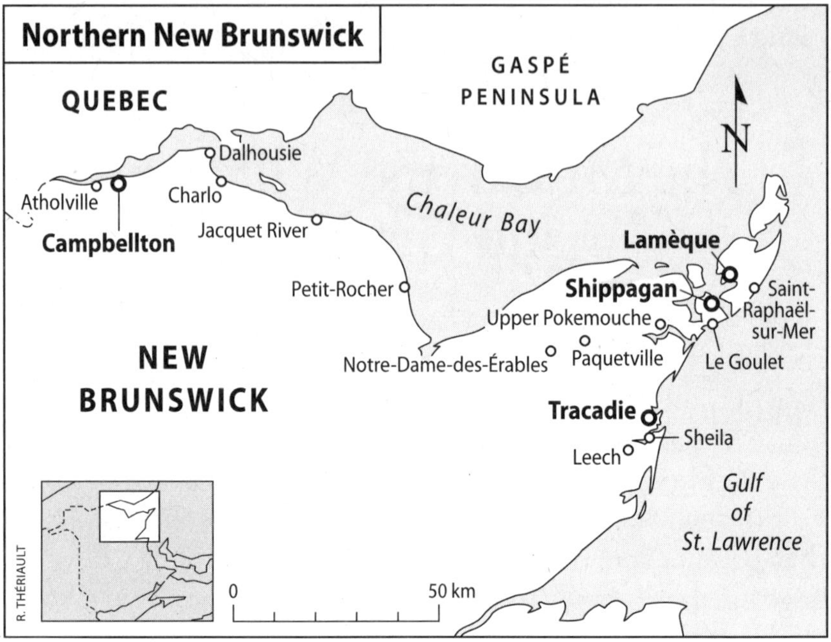


Aristide LeBlanc, from Cap-Pelé, New Brunswick, also talks about parents using the Mi-Carême as a way of making their children settle down. In the 1930s, he used to disguise himself on Mi-Carême to scare the children when they got out of school: "They'd see me and they'd be frightened. Well, that took care of them, then they wouldn't be as wild for a bit. They'd met the Mi-Carême."[56] Alyre Landry, from Notre-Dame, New Brunswick, recalls with a bit of humour: "We were good [around the middle of Lent]. During the summer, though, we'd forget about the Mi-Carême, then we'd get rambunctious again."[57]

Marie Robichaud from Saint-Charles, New Brunswick, was in the habit of using the Mi-Carême to make threats such as, "If you don't keep quiet, the Mi-Carêmes will come and get you,

56. CEA, Rose Robichaud Collection, Recording 7. See also Catherine Jolicoeur Collection, Recording 7,313.

57. CEA, Catherine Jolicoeur Collection, Recording 10,419.

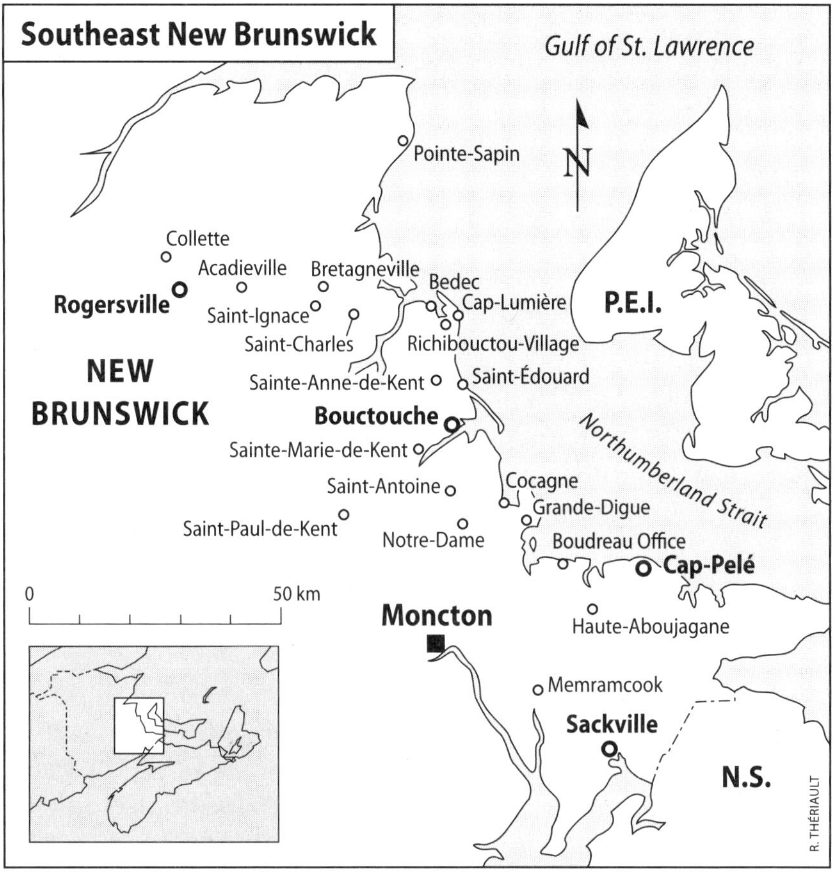


they'll put you in their bag."[58] One day, one of her children was so surprised and terrified by a Mi-Carême that he "nearly died." To calm him, Marie was forced to ask the Mi-Carême in question to take off her mask so her little boy could see whose face the mask was hiding. Afterwards, she never dared frighten her children like that again: "It had an effect on me, so I never scared them again."

In Jacket River, in northern New Brunswick, Herman Roy told the folklorist Sister Catherine Jolicoeur that when he was a child, people used to say that the Mi-Carême was a big beast

58. CEA, Catherine Jolicoeur Collection, Recording 12,791.

of some kind. As he explains, there was a drawing of a horse's head on his mother's Singer sewing machine: "My mother used to say it was the Mi-Carême. We were scared that that thing would come and get us if we were bad."[59]

The Mi-Carême also served as the bogeyman in many families on Prince Edward Island. Aubin "Joe" Perry, from St. Edward, remembers that his parents pretended that the Mi-Carême would hide in the attic and that she would come and take the children away if they did not obey.[60] He admits that even after he was older, his legs often shook with fear when he went upstairs. When Dennis Pitre was growing up in Tignish Shore, he imagined that the Mi-Carême lived in the woods not far from his home: "When I was young I always thought she lived over there in the woods, that she'd come out of the woods."[61] When he and the other children wanted to play in the woodlot, his mother, who was actually afraid they would get lost, used to say to them, "Don't go in the woods, the Mi-Carême will catch you."

Methods of controlling children have evolved over the years. Nowadays, parents have access to innumerable books with excellent advice on how to bring up their offspring. I have consulted these publications but not a single one of them recommends using the Mi-Carême or any other individual of that kind for disciplining children. Other days, other ways!

59. CEA, Catherine Jolicoeur Collection, Recording 17,464.

60. Georges Arsenault Collection, ms. 262.

61. Georges Arsenault Collection.

# The Mi-Carême, an Acadian Stork

In some Acadian regions, the Mi-Carême played an important role that had nothing to do with celebrating Mid-Lent or disciplining children. She was the one, supposedly, who brought babies. She does not seem to have had a monopoly on the task since traditions appear to have varied somewhat from one family to the next. In Sainte-Marie-de-Kent, New Brunswick, as in other villages, parents had various ways of explaining to their children how a newborn baby arrived: "We used to say it was the old [midwife] or Baby Jesus who delivered it, or that it fell from the sky, or that a woman from down the road left it, or that somebody found it under a rock, by a stream, in the warming oven, in Lazare's bog, or that the Mi-Carême left it. In later years, we used to say it was ordered from the Eaton's catalogue."[62] In many Acadian families, children were led to believe that Indians brought newborn babies.

The Acadians in northern New Brunswick, in the Gaspé Peninsula, on the Magdalen Islands, and on the North Shore of Quebec were the ones who relied the most on the Mi-Carême to deliver their babies.[63] It is important to note that this Acadian version of the stork was not the least bit kind; the mere mention of her name would frighten or terrorize children. When

62. Emery LeBlanc, *La vie à Sainte-Marie*, n.p., 1984, p. 59. See also Jean-Claude Dupont, *Héritage d'Acadie*, Montreal: Leméac, 1977, p. 150.

63. The doctor and writer Jacques Ferron says that he witnessed the tradition in the Northern Gaspé. See: "La Mi-Carême" in *L'information médicale et paramédicale*, Montreal: 18 January 1972, p. 20. It was this tradition that inspired his short story "La mi-carême," published in Jacques Ferron, *Contes*, édition intégrale, Montreal: Éditions HMH, 1970, pp. 66–7.

a woman was about to give birth, children were told that the Mi-Carême would be coming to see their mother. While this cruel, nasty stranger was visiting their home, children had to take refuge in the neighbour's house. When they came back home after the birth, they saw the baby but noticed that their mother was bedridden. The reason, so they were told, was because the Mi-Carême had mistreated her and, as a way of seeking forgiveness, she had given her a little baby.

Marie-Élizabeth Vautour from Campbellton, New Brunswick, who was born at the turn of the twentieth century, recalls what a dramatic event the Mi-Carême's visit was. "When a woman was about to have a baby, we were sent next door: 'Okay, the Mi-Carême's coming with a little baby. Come along all of you, we're going over to the neighbour's.' When we got there we hid. I was always easily frightened. There was no way I'd be at the window looking over at our house. Then we'd go back home. Our mother was sick in bed. The Mi-Carême had broken her leg and given her a baby. Of course, we didn't know any better."[64] Children had a hard time conjuring up an image of this malicious person, not knowing whether he or she was an animal or a human being. This ambiguity did nothing to reassure Germaine Le Breton Jean, a little girl in Paquetville:

> Imagine how scared and worried we were leaving Mom to be mistreated by that beast. We had no idea what a Mi-Carême looked like. All we knew was that it had a big stick and that it broke Mom's legs every time it came to the house. That's why Mom couldn't walk for several days after the delivery. That's quite a story to tell a five-year-old child! It stayed in our heads for a lot longer than the story about Santa Claus.[65]

---

64. CEA, Catherine Jolicoeur Collection, Recording 16,338.

65. Germaine Le Breton Jean, *Mon témoignage. Mon héritage.* Moncton: Éditions de la Francophonie, 2004, p. 61.

Irène Breau, from Comeau Settlement on the Acadian Peninsula, recalls that the Mi-Carême who brought babies to her house was invisible. "When we asked my grandmother if we could go and see the baby, she'd say, 'Wait until I get rid of the Mi-Carême.' Then she'd open the window and we'd hear her fall. There were fifteen of us. So there were lots of us to go out and watch the Mi-Carême leave, but we never saw her."[66] Other children managed to conjure up a very clear picture of this person, especially if they happened to see their father arrive with the midwife. Naturally they thought she was the Mi-Carême. Catherine Savoie, from Lamèque, New Brunswick, relates that "one time, we were at one of my uncle's places. We were looking out the window to watch for the Mi-Carême. My father arrived with her; she was an old woman wearing a dark black shawl. She went inside the house. We said to each other, 'Goodness, what's she going to do to Mom? Maybe she's going to eat her.' We were crying. We were looking out the windows over towards our place. We wanted to hurry back to see what had happened."[67]

Children often wondered where the woman who brought babies came from. Exilda Doucet's parents in Petit-Rocher said the Mi-Carême lived in the well with all the newborn babies. One day, Exilda and her little brother decided to go look in the well to see for themselves whether the Mi-Carême really lived there. "We went over to the well. Then we started throwing rocks in it and shouting to tell the big fat Mi-Carême to get out of there with those little babies, to bring them to us, that she didn't have any right to keep little babies in the dark, at the bottom of a well."[68] Since there was no response from the bottom of the well, the brave youngsters went away disappointed, seriously questioning their parents' word.

66. Georges Arsenault Collection.

67. CEA, Berthe Ferron Collection. Recording 15.

68. CEA, Jeanne Doucet Collection, Recording 22.

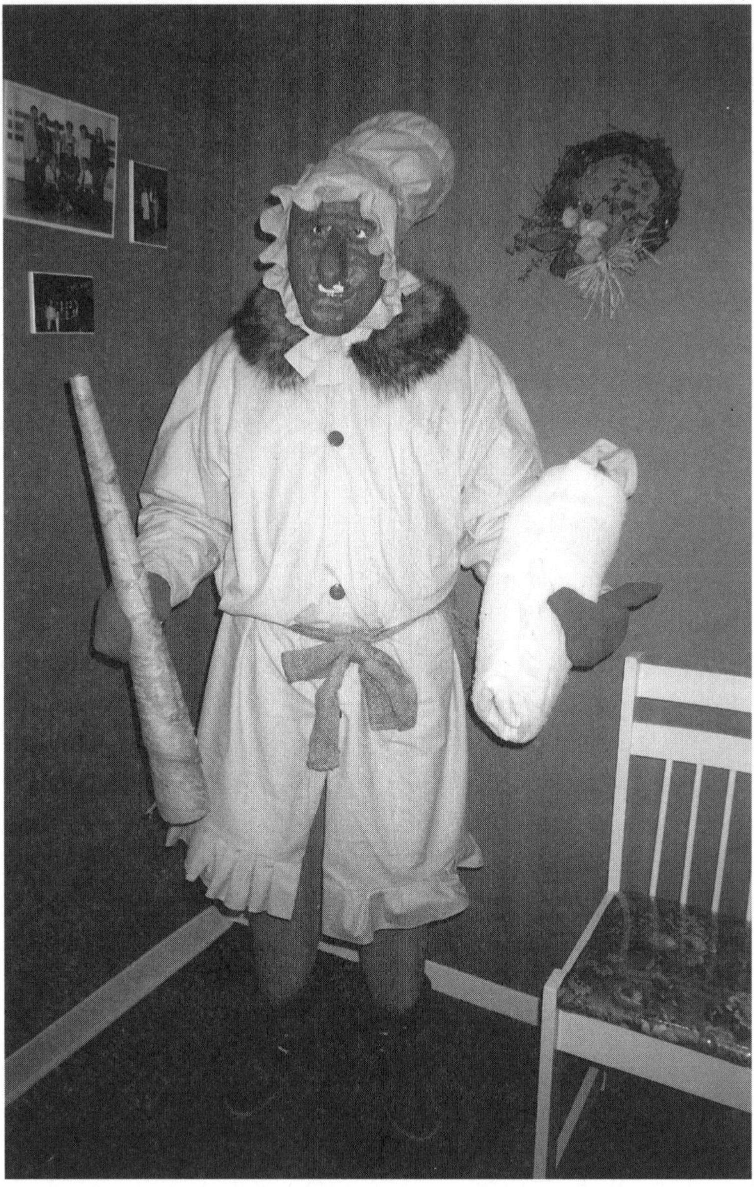

**The arrival of a new baby.** In 1997, Pierre Landry went masquerading at Mi-Carême in Natashquan, Quebec, pretending to be the Mi-Carême who used to deliver babies to the families in his village. He is holding the infant wrapped in swaddling clothes in one hand, and in the other a stick to break the mother's leg! (Bérangère Landry Collection)

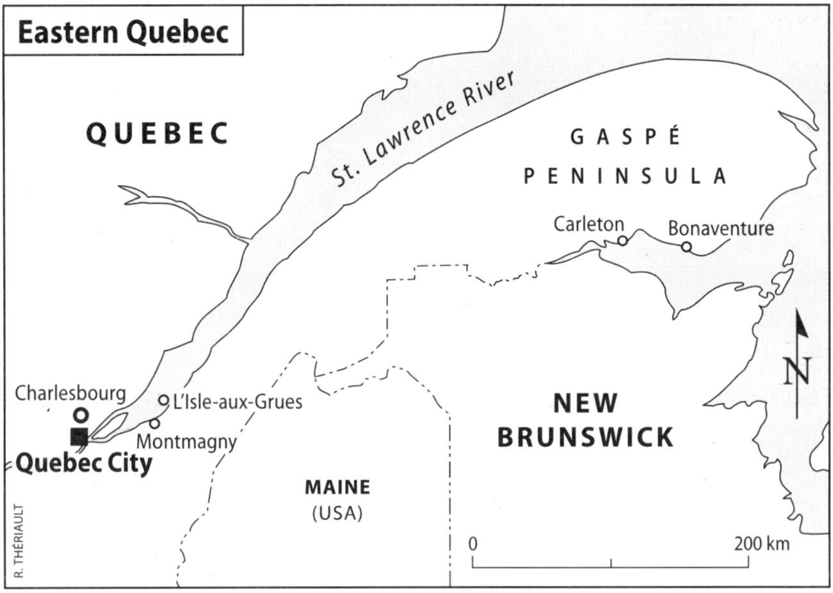


The Mi-Carême must have had a busy schedule, especially in the springtime when animals were giving birth, because in addition to bringing babies, she was also responsible for the delivery of calves, colts, lambs, and other farm animals. According to Gilbert LeBreton, in Tracadie, New Brunswick, "At calving time, we'd say that the Mi-Carêmes would be coming. Children weren't allowed in the barn. We'd cover up the windows with grey bags so they couldn't see in."[69]

The adults in Rolande Lamarche's home in Saint-Quentin, in northern New Brunswick, used to say that the Mi-Carême was a big hunchback with a beard who walked around with a huge bag for gathering up children. He would take them back home, cook them, and eat them! This grotesque character always carried a little crutch and a hammer. Whenever a cow was going to calve, Rolande Lamarche's father would leave a big bag, a hammer, and a crutch, made from a tree root, outside the barn. When the children saw those things, it was a sure

69. CEA, Carmen LeBreton Collection, ms. 8.

sign that the Mi-Carême was around somewhere, maybe even in the stable, which meant they had to take off; otherwise, they risked being snatched away.[70]

It has been a long time since the Mi-Carême has brought babies and newborn animals to Acadian families. She gradually lost those duties as modern medicine started taking over deliveries, first with a house call from the doctor, and then with the hospitalization of the mother. Children were told that the doctor brought the baby or that their Mom had found it at the hospital. Nowadays, giving birth is no longer shrouded in mystery. Every child knows that the baby grows in a mother's tummy and that baby animals grow in their mothers' bellies. Stories about the Mi-Carême, bearer of babies, are gradually disappearing from the Acadians' collective memory. Unlike the famous stork, she never had the opportunity to appear on commercial greeting cards announcing births and reminding us of ancient traditions.

70. CEA, Gordon Boulay Collection, Recording 1,173.

# Making House-Visits

Of all the Acadian traditions related to Mid-Lent, the group activity of going from house to house or "running the Mi-Carême" was and is still the most popular. Once known in many Acadian villages in the Maritimes and in the province of Quebec, this masquerade has declined considerably since the 1960s. Today, the only region in the Maritimes where the tradition is practised is Chéticamp, Nova Scotia; and, in Quebec, the only Acadian villages where it is still alive are Fatima, on the Magdalen Islands, and Natashquan, on the North Shore. Aside from these Acadian communities, masquerading at Mi-Carême is still common in L'Isle-aux-Grues, a little community located in the St. Lawrence River, not far from Montmagny, Quebec.[71]

Mi-Carême was not the only occasion when Acadians would put on masks and go from door to door. In some regions, it was done as a way of collecting food on 2 February for Candlemas. This custom was common in southern New Brunswick; on Prince Edward Island; in Cape Breton; on the Magdalen Islands; and the Port-au-Port Peninsula in Newfoundland.[72] In the northern part of New Brunswick and in the Acadian villages of Quebec, people used to put on costumes to collect for Mardi Gras, a custom still practised enthusiastically by the Cajuns in Louisiana.[73] The Franco-Acadians on the west coast

---

71. Pierre Dunnigan and Francine Saint-Laurent, *Mi-Carême. Une fête québécoise à redécouvrir*, Montreal: Les 400 coups, 2006, pp. 31–60.

72. Georges Arsenault, *Courir la Chandeleur*, Moncton: Éditions d'Acadie, 1982, 116 p.

73. Jean-Claude Dupont, *op. cit.*, pp. 288–99; Anne-Marie Desdouits, *op. cit.*, pp. 158–62; Jeanne Pomerleau, *Corvées et quêtes. Un parcours au Canada français*, Montreal: Hurtubise HMH, 2002, pp. 355–66; Barry Jean Ancelet, Jay Edwards and Glen Pitre, *Cajun Country*, Jackson: University Press of Mississippi, 1991, pp. 84–94.

**In the land of snow.** These warmly dressed Mi-Carêmes were making their rounds in Bedec, New Brunswick, in 1960. Obviously, there was no lack of snow that year. (Claudette and Roger Richard Collection)

of Newfoundland have adopted the Irish and English tradition of mummering, very similar to the Mi-Carême masquerade, which is carried out between Christmas and Epiphany (6 January).[74] In the 1950s and 1960s, with the growing popularity and commercialization of Halloween, Acadians everywhere began getting dressed up to go out trick or treating. Prior to that, 31 October was simply known as *la veille de la Toussaint* (the eve of All Saints' Day) or *le soir des tours* (the

74. Gary R. Butler, *Histoire et traditions orales des Franco-Acadiens de Terre-Neuve*, Sillery: Septentrion, 1995, p. 70; Gerald Thomas, "Noël, la Chandeleur, Mardi gras. Begging Rituals in French Newfoundland," *Fields of Folklore.* Essays in Honor of Kenneth S. Goldstein, ed. Roger D. Abrahams, Bloomington: Trickster Press, 1995, pp. 300–9. For information on the mummering tradition in Newfoundland and Labrador generally, see *Christmas Mumming in Newfoundland*, ed. Herbert Halpert and G. M. Story, Toronto: University of Toronto Press, 1990, 250 p.

**A little heat.** It is often very cold at Mi-Carême since it normally falls sometime in March. This masquerader in Chéticamp, Nova Scotia, is taking advantage of the warmth of the kitchen stove before moving on to the next house in the neighbourhood. (Centre de la Mi-Carême Collection)

evening of tricks). On that night, young people, not wearing masks, would go around surreptitiously playing harmless or sometimes nasty pranks on their neighbours.

In most Acadian regions, the masqueraders or Mi-Carêmes, as they were known, did not do any collecting as was done for Candlemas, Mardi Gras, and, in later years, for Halloween. They just went from door to door, trying not to be recognized by their hosts. If they were offered a treat or a drink of alcohol, they would accept it with pleasure and consume on the spot whatever refreshments they were given.

## News About Mi-Carême

**Corberrie, Nova Scotia** — On Wednesday evening, a group of about ten young people, dressed in disguises, paraded through the village of Corberrie to celebrate Mi-Carême. What a racket of drums, horns, pennywhistles, megaphones, bells, tambourines, etc. What a surprise for the little children who were all trembling at the sight of these walking ghosts.

(*L'Évangéline*, 28 March 1895)

**Sainte-Marie-de-Kent, New Brunswick** — There were quite a few Mi-Carêmes this year, all in clever disguises. They were even more joyful than in recent years; comical and a little noisy, they succeeded in entertaining us for a pleasant quarter of an hour. We thanked them for their visit that was too short. We invited them to come back again next year.

(*L'Évangéline*, 3 April 1930)

**Bretagneville, New Brunswick** — A number of "Mi-Carêmes" came visiting this year. Some of them were from Africa, Florida, etc.

(*L'Évangéline*, 22 March 1934)

**New Waterford, Cape Breton, Nova Scotia** — Our young Acadians followed the old customs and enjoyed themselves a lot at Mi-Carême.

(*L'Évangéline*, 29 March 1934)

**Saint-Édouard, New Brunswick** — The "Mi-Carêmes" visited us on the 27th and 28th. They came from everywhere and there were all different kinds.

(*L'Évangéline*, 4 April 1935)

**Saint-Joseph-du-Moine, Cape Breton, Nova Scotia** — The young people in our parish celebrated Mi-Carême enthusiastically this week. It is an old custom that never fails to amuse both those who masquerade and those who try to guess who is behind the mask.

(*L'Évangéline*, 4 April 1935)

**Saint-Thomas de Kent, New Brunswick** — The weather has been very cold since the beginning of March, but there is no snow. All the young people are getting ready to go out masquerading for Mi-Carême.

(*L'Évangéline*, 16 March 1939)

**Belle Côte, Nova Scotia** — An even bigger band of masqueraders made its usual round for Mi-Carême. The characters were of various ages, dressed in a variety of disguises, and came from everywhere, representing several nationalities.

(*L'Évangéline*, 10 April 1941)

**Cap-aux-Meules, Madgalen Islands, Quebec** — Mi-Carême has come and gone, and so have the Mi-Carêmes. Like everything else, their costumes show signs of change. We saw some in the streets of Cap-aux-Meules who were really impressive. There were animals; Indian chiefs with their headdress blowing in the wind; and minstrels playing some lively reels on the guitar or the fiddle to pay for the hospitality. These popular celebrations serve a function and are thoroughly appreciated by the public when they respect both property and individuals and even more so when they are tainted with civility as was the case this year.

(*La Boussole*, 1 April 1957)

The custom of masquerading and making house-visits, well honoured in both Quebec and the Maritimes, no doubt originated in France. It may well have been a vibrant tradition in western France when Acadie and Quebec were colonized, but it appears to have been more or less abandoned since it is rarely mentioned by folklorists and writers documenting traditions in France at the end of the nineteenth century and the first half of the twentieth. However, the ethnologist Anne-Marie Desdouits discovered during her research in the Pays de Caux in Upper Normandy, around 1980, that the custom of masquerading at Mi-Carême was well-known at the beginning of the twentieth century, but that it was reserved for children. They would disguise themselves and walk around the streets, sometimes knocking on doors for pancakes, doughnuts, or coins.[75] Prior to the twentieth century, in all likelihood, this type of masquerade would have been common for men in many areas of France. In his *Manuel de folklore français contemporain*, Arnold Van Gennep, the renowned expert of French folklore, states that the tradition of masqueraders going from house to house, like that of Mi-Carême, had declined considerably in France by the late 1800s:

> Most authors writing in the nineteenth century and the first quarter of the twentieth century, and virtually all of my direct witnesses, numbering approximately 2,000, indicated that disguises customary "in the olden days" disappeared fairly quickly after the wars of 1870 and 1914–1918, and that "in the olden days" even adults took part in this form of entertainment and the pranks that went with it, but that little by little it was limited to young people of both sexes, and then to children after 1920; so that disguises disappeared from streets and public places, more or less quickly depending on the region, and only appeared in the form of "masked balls" in enclosed locations.[76]

---

75. Anne-Marie Desdouits, *op. cit.*, p. 174.

76. Arnold Van Gennep, *op. cit.*, p. 883.

**On to the next house.** Several Mi-Carêmes leave a house in Wellington to continue their house-visits in the Evangeline region, Prince Edward Island, in 1981. (Georges Arsenault Collection)

These masked balls were already part of Mi-Carême festivities by the middle of the nineteenth century in urban areas of Normandy. The novelist Gustave Flaubert gives a dramatic portrait of this form of celebration in *Madame Bovary*, published in 1857. The action takes place near Rouen, Flaubert's birthplace. On Mi-Carême, Emma, the famous heroine, disguises herself as a man and spends all night at a masked ball. "The Thursday night of the mi-carême—the mid-Lenten festivities—she didn't return to Yonville, but went to a masked ball. She wore velvet knee breeches and red stockings and a peruke, and a cocked hat over one ear. She danced all night to the wild sound of trombones; she was the centre of an admiring throng..."[77]

77. Gustave Flaubert, *Madame Bovary*, New York: Random House, new translation by Francis Steegmuller, 1957, pp. 330–1.

Van Gennep's observations could also apply to masquerades in French Canada, except that on this side of the Atlantic, the popularity of the masquerades associated with Chandeleur, Mardi Gras, and Mi-Carême did not really begin to wane until after the Second World War and more specifically after the Second Vatican Ecumenical Council (1962–65). Masquerading and making house-visits was originally the prerogative of men, although in most Acadian villages, as we shall see, children and young people of both sexes gradually joined the festivities. In many areas, the term "little" Mi-Carême was used to describe a child who masqueraded and the term "big" or "tall" Mi-Carême referred to adults.

# Dressed in Rags and Tatters

Like the Mi-Carême who distributed candies to children, the masqueraders or Mi-Carêmes who went around the neighbourhood in groups were anything but beautiful. When you got disguised as a Mi-Carême, you usually made a point of looking strange, eccentric, ugly, or even hideous. If by chance you did go to the trouble of making a special costume, it was done without ado and at little cost, as was the case when Marie-Colombe Robichaud was growing up in Chéticamp, Nova Scotia, in the 1940s and 1950s:

> The Mi-Carêmes made their own costumes. There were no stores where you could rent costumes and masks. We used old nylon stockings, pillowcases, or cardboard to cover our faces. We'd root around in trunks and suitcases for old clothes. We'd add lots of colour by sewing pieces of cloth on old used clothing. We'd also add bits of jewellery and have things like bells and horns to make lots of noise.[78]

In most Acadian communities, costumes for Mi-Carêmes were improvised from old clothes. If there was any chance that someone would recognize them, they were simply turned inside out. If you wanted to remain incognito, you had to watch what you chose for a disguise. Always anxious to guess the identity of the masqueraders, the hosts made a point of examining their clothes for any clues. It would be easy to recognize the navy blue coat somebody's father had worn for ten years or the hat somebody's grandmother had been wearing to church ever since the founding of the parish. If you were lucky, you

78. Georges Arsenault Collection, ms. 278.

could disguise yourself with used clothes that had been sent by relatives in the United States and that nobody would recognize. In those days, almost every Acadian had family members who had emigrated to New England to find work. Every year, you received big boxes or barrels of clothes that were no longer needed or that had been bought in rummage sales. Joe Delaney, from Saint-Joseph-du-Moine, Nova Scotia, recalls that a barrel could hold "about a dozen pairs of shoes, 2 or 3 suits, a coat, half a dozen shirts, some sweaters."[79] He says that the clothes that were set aside for Mi-Carême were ones that nobody wanted to wear because they did not correspond to the local style. Édith Comeau-Tufts, a Nova Scotian Acadian from Saulnierville, also remembers how important those American barrels were at Mi-Carême: "We'd get together in someone's house, then we'd look through the clothes in the barrel. We'd all find something that nobody would've seen, we'd be wearing old clothes from the States. Nobody would be able to say that it was your sister's dress, or that it was... They were nice outfits. You had to be careful not to tear them because the families that had received the clothes would eventually be using them."[80]

Women's clothing often served as disguises for men and boys, while women and girls got decked out in clothes for the opposite sex. This sex reversal made it more difficult to be recognized. There was never any lack of imagination. The burlap from potato bags was recycled for a costume. Some masqueraders would stuff their jackets and pants with straw; others would turn into hunchbacks with the help of a cushion under their coats. Rope was used to make wigs or beards. In Charlos Cove, Nova Scotia, it was not uncommon to make a costume with birch bark attached to burlap or cardboard. People who wore

79. Interviews done by Ron Caplan and edited with the help of Rosie Aucoin published in *Acadian Lives in Cape Breton Island*, Wreck Cove: Breton Books, 2004, p. 160.

80. Centre acadien, Université Sainte-Anne, Labor-Sébastien Dol Collection, Recording 68.

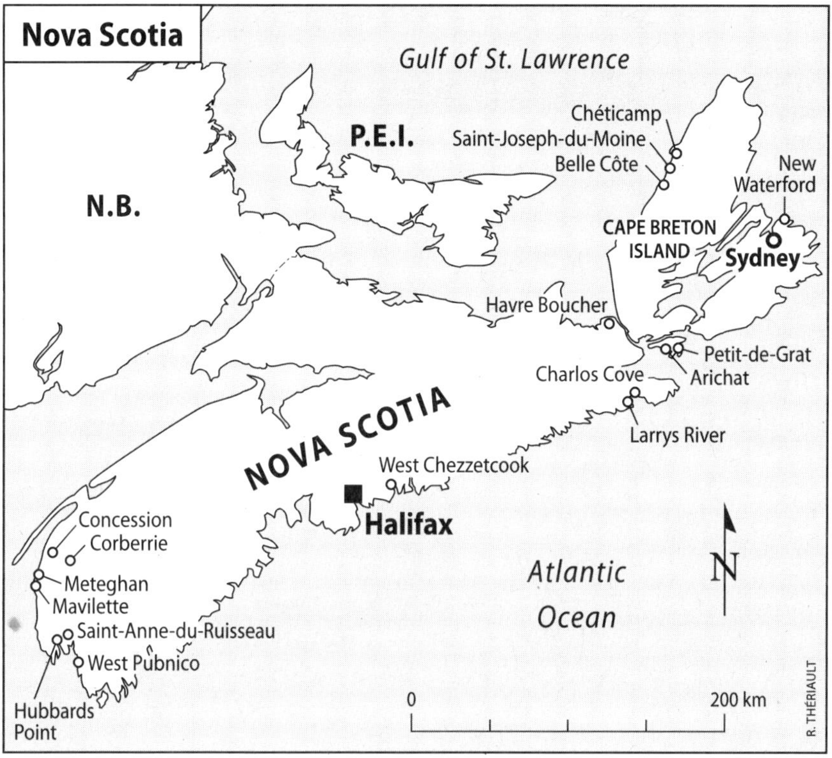


this disguise were called *les Mi-Carêmes des bois francs* (the Mi-Carêmes from the hardwood stands).[81] Generally, people gave free rein to their creativity so that there were almost as many different costumes as there were masqueraders.

Like today, the mask constituted an essential element of the disguise since it had to hide the face of the person playing the role of the Mi-Carême, while at the same time allowing him or her to see and to breathe. According to Joe Delaney, some people are even better than detectives at recognizing masqueraders. That is why you have to be sure everything is hidden: "You've got to sort of have a cloth-like over, before you put on your mask — hide all your hair, your ears, and the side of the

81. Georges Arsenault Collection, ms. 272. Informant: Fran (Richard) Campbell.

## In Rags and Tatters

"We'd get dressed in old clothes and go from house to house. Then we'd go to one particular place and dance all evening. Girls tended to dress as guys and boys like girls, so it was hard to tell who was who."

— **Estère McIntyre** (Charlo, New Brunswick)

"You'd hear them coming in the distance. The bells we had were made of tin, from cans; we'd attach them right on us. We got dressed in bags, the ones for putting potatoes in. We used stuff like that. We made beards with rope, it was all braided. Things like that."

— **Aimé J. Larocque** (Saint-Raphaël-sur-Mer, New Brunswick)

"We used to save old clothes. We'd put them in the attic and then we'd get dressed in those things. Men usually put on women's clothes because that would disguise them better. Old dresses, old battered straw hats. All the things women wore. After they'd worn them, when they were too old, they'd put them up in the attic. Cotton stockings, because there was no nylon in those days. We'd put them over our face. They'd cover your head and your face. We'd cut out the eyes, the nose and the mouth. Those were our masks. The uglier, the better!"

— **Yvonne Comeau** (Meteghan, Nova Scotia)

"You were dressed in half an hour. A woman's old cap, a stocking over your face, some lipstick, an old dress, we'd add humps. Nothing more than that. A glove on one hand and a mitten on the other. We made masks out of cardboard. We'd take a bit of rope, big thick rope, we'd unravel it and then stick it on for a beard. We had old pipes, they were called corn cob pipes."

— **Roger Richard** (Bedec, New Brunswick)

"In the 40s, we got dressed up for Mi-Carême. We didn't pretend to be anything, it didn't take much time: a pillowcase, a nylon stocking pulled over your face, a sheet or an old blanket on your back, a coat turned inside out. Guys got disguised as women. People dressed with what they had: rags and tatters."

— **Claranda Landry** (Natashquan, Quebec)

"We disguised ourselves with old clothes we found in the attic. One thing that was very popular was my mother's old nylon stockings that we'd pull down over our head and face. Our costumes weren't nice, they were ugly, not like today's beautiful costumes that you buy in the big chain stores. I remember that we went around with our friends in little groups. I remember that it was often really cold; after all it was wintertime. We had to pile on lots of old clothes so we wouldn't freeze. During the rest of the year, whenever we saw people who were badly dressed, we'd call them Mi-Carêmes."

— **Normand Maillet** (Collette, New Brunswick)

**Masqueraders in Natashquan.** It is hard to find photos taken of Mi-Carêmes before 1950. This one, dated 1935, shows a group of young people in Natashquan, Quebec. Holding their sticks, all these Mi-Carêmes are just clad in old clothes, except for the one on the far left who is disguised as a cat. (Bernard Landry Collection)

face. So that once you put the mask on, there's no skin showing. Because some of them, they can guess — if they happen to see one eye, the end of the nose, an ear — right away, they've got you. Oh yeah, it's unbelievable."[82]

The most common masks were pulled down over the head and were easy to make: a cotton or nylon stocking, a pillowcase, or even the sleeve from a sweater or a man's undershirt. Scissors were used to cut holes for the eyes, the nose, and the mouth. Sometimes, they were outlined with lipstick. "We made masks with cardboard boxes," says Azade Mallet from Le Goulet, New Brunswick, and "blackened our eyes with charcoal. Other people used women's hats with [veils] over their

82. *Acadian Lives in Cape Breton Island, op. cit.*, pp. 160–1.

face."[83] Based on her research on Mid-Lenten traditions in the Gaspé Peninsula around 1950, the folklorist Carmen Roy states that masks were also made with things from the woods: "People used, and are still using, birch bark for making masks, hairy lichen from maple trees for false beards, and lobster claws for noses. We were also told that there were a few wooden masks (a pig's snout, etc.)."[84]

Yves Frenette remembers that in Petit Rocher, New Brunswick, small masks were sold at the store for seven or eight cents which people liked to fix up. "We changed them a little bit. We'd add some hair. I'd have to go out to the barn. I'd cut off the end of the calf's tail, and that was a mustache!"[85] Sometimes people just blackened their face with soot or some sort of polish.

Judging by the following description by the ethnologist Arnold Van Gennep, if Acadian Mi-Carêmes had wanted to prolong their annual visits by going back to the land of their ancestors, they would have felt at home among French masqueraders:

> The process for disguising oneself in rural areas was simple: one merely blackened one's face with polish or soot; for the costume, one exchanged clothes depending on the sex, men usually put on women's long petticoats whereas the women got dressed in trousers and jackets turned inside out; goat skin is also mentioned frequently since it enables one to look like a bear or any wild animal. Young men willingly put on women's bonnets, and girls donned cotton bonnets, felt hats, or caps.[86]

---

83. CEA, Marlène Roussel Collection, ms. 1.
84. Carmen Roy, "Le carnaval-carême en Gaspésie," *Bulletin No. 125 du Musée national du Canada pour l'année financière 1951–1952*, Ottawa, 1953, p. 96.
85. CEA, Lauraine Léger Collection, Recording 2035.
86. Arnold Van Gennep, *op. cit.*, pp. 883–4.

Acadian Mi-Carêmes could also have passed unnoticed among the mummers of Newfoundland at Christmastime, since their disguises were very similar.[87]

As in France, the Mi-Carêmes sometimes disguised themselves with real animal skins. Evidence to that effect has been collected in several Acadian regions. "I remember," relates Pamphile Bouchard from the Magdalen Islands, "that we covered our whole body with an old skin from an animal like a bull. We'd use the skin from the head to cover up our face completely. We'd try to keep the horns so we'd be as horned as the devil! We could see through the holes where the eyes of the animal had been taken out!"[88] Zita Allain, from Saint-Antoine, New Brunswick, who was 91 years old in 1977, remembers a man in her village, by the name of Aurèle à Octave à Zaï, who spent a great deal of energy making his costume for Mi-Carême. "In the fall, they killed a big cow with black and white spots. He removed the skin and let it dry properly. He left the horns on. He went out dressed in that. He had a bell around his neck. He came into the house on all fours, with the bell and the horns. It looked exactly like a cow. He was wearing the cow skin on his body."[89]

This tradition appears to have been more common on the Gaspé side of Chaleur Bay. In that region, where there is a high concentration of Acadians, masqueraders would sometimes put on the skin from a bear or a farm animal.[90] Fernand Arsenault remembers very clearly the troupe that invaded his family home in Bonaventure in the early 1930s when he was a little boy: "The little door was ajar and through the crack I could see men's big legs covered in animal skins, long cow tails

87. Herbert Halpert and G. M. Story, *op.cit.* See, in particular, the chapter by J. D. A. Widdowson and Herbert Halpert entitled "The Disguises of Newfoundland Mummers," pp. 145–64.

88. Quoted in Pierre Dunnigan and Francine Saint-Laurent, *op. cit.*, p. 27.

89. CEA, Lauraine Léger Collection, Recording 1200.

90. Carmen Roy, *loc. cit.*, pp. 95–6.

**They're funny-looking Mi-Carêmes!** Young Robert MacFarland (left) is obviously enjoying these four young Mi-Carêmes making their rounds in Chéticamp. The photo was taken by Robert's mother, Inez H. MacFarland, in 1941. (Robert MacFarland Collection)

dragging on the floor, and sticks hammering the beat of songs and dances. Looking over the top of the door, I could distinguish faces that were half man, half bull, heads with big horns, strange and very ugly characters."[91] The men in Bonaventure eventually abandoned their annual rounds, but young boys, led by Fernand Arsenault, took over the tradition. Instead of covering themselves with animal skins, they just got dressed in rags and made masks that looked like animal heads.

On Isle Madame, Nova Scotia, the masqueraders in the early 1900s were more stylish, at least if they were well-to-do. According to Sister Catherine Gagnon from Arichat, "some got dressed up as very rich people, others as clowns, others as

91. Fernand Arsenault, "La Mi-Carême," manuscript.

women or young girls."[92] People thought nothing of buying beautiful cloth at the store to make fancy costumes. In this case, recycling took place in reverse order: once the masquerade was over, the material from the costumes was used to make ordinary clothes. "The costumes were made with calico, bought especially for the occasion," recalls Sister Marie Boucher. "It was reused for more suitable, more practical clothing."[93] According to Narcisse Marchand, from Petit-de-Grat, you could make a nice clown costume with five yards of material. "In those days, it cost ten cents a yard for the best calico you could buy. Oh, what beautiful calico. After you'd finished being a Mi-Carême, your mother or someone else would make beautiful quilts with it."

In several villages along the coast of Kent County, New Brunswick, masqueraders in the 1940s and 1950s were also well-dressed, especially in Bouctouche and Richibouctou-Village. People went to a lot of trouble to make very attractive costumes, the most popular of which were decorated with crêpe paper of various colours. Crêpe paper was also used to decorate high hats made from cardboard especially for the occasion. In the little village of Bedec, some individuals liked to dress as specific characters. "Some years they dressed as jokers," recalls Roger Richard. "One time, they were disguised as policemen."[94] They stood out from the masqueraders from other villages because of their preference for fancy costumes: "You'd know they came from Bedec because of their costumes."[95] In 1952, the novelist and playwright Antonine Maillet taught in Richibouctou-Village, located near Bedec, where she no doubt witnessed these Mi-Carêmes masquerading as specific characters since they reappear several years later in her writings.

---

92. CEA, Hélène Robinson Collection, ms. 24.
93. CEA, Ginette Ste-Marie Collection, ms. 22.
94. CEA, Lauraine Léger Collection, Recording 1394.
95. CEA, Robert Richard Collection.

**An attractive, unmasked Mi-Carême.** Florida Maillet from Cap-Lumière, New Brunswick, is wearing the costume she made for herself in 1945. She sewed rows of different colour crêpe paper on her jacket and her trousers. (Hélène Allain Collection)

Her stay in Richibouctou-Village was the inspiration for her first novel, *Pointe-aux-Coques*, in which the heroine, a young Acadian teacher from New England, was introduced to the Mi-Carême masquerade. The schoolteacher was amazed by the originality and the variety of costumes: "Malvina's huge kitchen turned into a long waiting room with clowns, pirates, Eskimos, domino masks, and Punchinellos moving about. [...] When I got closer, I realized that these tunics, puffed sleeves, three-cornered hats, and Turkish slippers, had all been made with old cloth or burlap bags. For over ten days people have

**Three jokers in Bedec.** People in Bedec, New Brunswick, stood out at Mi-Carême because of their elaborate costumes. Aurèle, Albert, and Antoine Allain are the jokers. The photo was taken at Mi-Carême around 1952. (Claudette and Roger Richard Collection)

been busy sewing and dyeing."[96] In fact, costumes were made over a period of several days, even several weeks. "In Fond-de-la-Baie and in Sainte-Anne," recalls Lucille Daigle, "I'm sure those folks worked for many months before Mi-Carême to make their costumes."[97]

These characters from Isle Madame and Kent County with their elaborate costumes are the forerunners of the wonderful Mi-Carêmes that are now the norm in Chéticamp, Fatima, Natashquan, and L'Isle-aux-Grues. The masqueraders in those places have become quite stylish. They have long since abandoned animal skins and rarely dress in old rags or clothes turned inside out. Their masks, much more sophisticated than in the past, come from faraway countries and are purchased in the local stores. Sometimes, they are even created by local artists. In the final analysis, the Mi-Carêmes have moved with the times. They have been influenced by the styles of the day, advertisements, and marketing. Sometimes a masquerader even has the nerve to come dressed up as a famous Hollywood star or a prime minister! If you are badly dressed, Acadians say that you are "dressed like a Mi-Carême." It is a fair bet, however, that that disparaging comment will soon lose its original meaning.

96. Antonine Maillet, *Pointe-aux-Coques*, Montreal: Leméac, 1972 (original edition 1958), p. 103. According to Antonine Maillet, in all likelihood the carnival that was organized on the outdoor skating rink in Bouctouche between 1930 and 1940 influenced the Mi-Carême costumes in the Bedec area of Kent County. During this winter festival that took place in February, there was rivalry to see who had the most beautiful and most sophisticated costume. According to Maillet, the Mi-Carême masqueraders in Bouctouche and the surrounding area only used old clothes for their costumes. Source: telephone conversation with the author, 13 September 2007.

97. CEA, Robert Richard Collection.

# Adults Make Their Rounds

Based on the evidence I have gathered, it would appear that for a long time masquerading at Mi-Carême was the exclusive prerogative of men. In some villages, women only started making house-visits at Mi-Carême in the early 1900s. In many regions, however, right up until the annual tradition disappeared, the adult or "big" Mi-Carêmes were always men. In 1982, when she was 91 years old, Belzémée Babineau, from Acadieville, New Brunswick, stated, "It would have been frowned upon to send girls out running around on Mi-Carême."[98] On the other hand, girls were not indifferent to the masqueraders, especially since they were often the target of the guys who looked forward to teasing them and above all dancing with them. Régina Savoie, living in Atholville, New Brunswick, but born in Carleton on the Gaspé Peninsula, says that the masqueraders "wanted the girl in the house to dance with them, but she didn't want to dance because they looked like devils."[99] Not all young girls tried to avoid the masqueraders. On the contrary, they would get together sometimes in a particular house to greet them. According to Wilfred Cordeau, on Isle Madame, Nova Scotia, the guys were sure to have fun in that house and would take advantage of the opportunity to set up a rendezvous with the girls over the next few days.[100]

98. CEA, François Bessette Collection, ms. 11.

99. Archives de folklore et d'ethnologie de l'Université Laval (AFEUL), Catherine Jolicoeur Collection, Recording 192.

100. CEA, Jocelyne Marchand Collection, Recording 89.

Young men who were shy or not in the habit of approaching girls obviously felt much braver when they were wearing masks. Johnny Boudreau, from Petit-Rocher, New Brunswick, made house-visits on Mi-Carême around 1930. "As for us, when we went to a house where there were girls, we weren't shy. We went in, then we danced. Yes, I think we felt less embarrassed. Otherwise we'd have never done that."[101] According to another New Brunswicker, Anselme Mallet, from Shippagan, when boys spotted girls to their liking, they would eagerly await Mi-Carême for the chance to kiss them. When they arrived at the young lady's home and after they had been given permission to enter, they would take turns giving her a kiss. "And would you believe it," said Mr. Mallet, "the young girls didn't mind that at all!"[102]

In the 1930s on Isle Madame, girls eventually began putting on masks and going out on Mi-Carême with the guys. According to Evelyne Boudreau, that was what contributed to the disappearance of the tradition in the early 1940s. "In the end, it was all the same because girls started getting disguised at Mi-Carême. So there were no more girls in the houses to see them. It was foolish to have started doing that. I did it myself one year."[103]

The way the "big" Mi-Carêmes made their rounds varied somewhat, depending on the village and the years. Generally, however, Acadian Mi-Carêmes were similar in that they were all joyful and high-spirited. Their visit provided a temporary break in the long, dreary peacefulness of Lent. Dressed in strange costumes and armed with canes, bells, noisemakers, and makeshift drums, they went from one end of the village to the other on foot, by sleigh, and eventually by car. When they arrived at a house, the revellers would knock on the door,

101. CEA, Lauraine Léger Collection, Recording 1973.
102. CEA, Chantal Duguay Collection, ms. 13.
103. CEA, Jocelyne Marchand Collection, Recording 70.

**Handsome masks.** This photo was taken in Saint-Joseph-du-Moine, Nova Scotia, in the 1930s. It is clear that the masks of these Mi-Carêmes were homemade. The long beard of one of the masqueraders was probably made from rope. (Centre de la Mi-Carême Collection)

something only strangers used to do. Louise Comeau has not forgotten the masqueraders who went from house to house in Meteghan River, Nova Scotia. "Several groups came by the same evening and they knocked on the door saying, 'Will you let the Mi-Carêmes in?' It was amazing to hear a knock at the door because people walked in without ever knocking. Only strangers or the English knocked."[104] Élise Cormier, from Sainte-Marie-de-Kent, New Brunswick, states, "We used a cane to announce our presence. If they didn't let us in, we'd have knocked even harder, but they always let us in. They weren't frightened because they knew it was people from the area."[105] Once the Mi-Carêmes had permission, they would burst noisily into the kitchen where the members of the family were

104. Georges Arsenault Collection, ms. 281.

105. CEA, Yves Cormier Collection, ms. 8.

*Illustration: Denise Paquette*

gathered together. Little children would cling with terror to their mother's apron or hide as best they could in a corner or take refuge in another room where they could watch in safety the antics of these frightening visitors. Diane Nadeau, from L'Étang-du-Nord on the Magdalen Islands, relates that her first encounters with Mi-Carêmes, when she was about four years old, were quite terrifying. "One evening, about seven o'clock, three people in disguises knocked at the door; my mother told them to come in. As soon as I saw them I started to cry, then I went and hid in the living room until they left. For the next two years, I had the same problem each time. I was so scared that I had bad dreams for a week or more."[106]

The adults and older children would peer at each of the masqueraders, hoping to discover their identities. They would ask them questions like: Have you come from far away? What's

106. CEA, Diane Nadeau Collection, ms. 3.

your name? Can you dance? Are you hungry? They would answer by nodding their heads and gesturing with their hands. If they dared speak, they would change their voices and only say a few words. If they were too chatty, they risked giving themselves away. When a Mi-Carême was recognized, he would take off his mask, then he was "handed a treat." That is how it took place in Clara Dugas's home in Saint Mary's Bay, Nova Scotia. "Our parents and my grandmother tried to guess who the characters were. They'd look at their hands, their boots, and their funny clothes. Everybody would be laughing. If they guessed, the masks would be taken off joyfully, then they'd be offered a piece of rappie pie, some tea or rum, and always some fudge."[107]

Music was normally an essential part of the masqueraders' visit. There was usually one fellow who had a harmonica in his pocket so his joyful companions could dance. Houses where there were musicians were always appreciated whether it was a fiddler, a mouth-organist, an accordionist, or even just someone who could jig the tunes of reels for the dancing. In Lamèque, New Brunswick, the Mi-Carêmes would stop at Célestin Chiasson's place. "My father was a fiddler," relates Aurèle Chiasson. "When the Mi-Carêmes came to the house, the Mi-Carêmes would say, 'Célestin, will you play us a jig?' Some of the gang could step-dance. Well, Célestin would play a tune on the fiddle, then the Mi-Carêmes would dance. The dancing would last for a little while. Then they'd move on."[108] In some homes, the hosts would only distribute rewards after the visitors had finished their improvised performance. Around 1930 in Meteghan River, Nova Scotia, the masqueraders who went around the village made a point of having a fiddler so they could do a square dance. "It was understood," recalls Yvonne Comeau, "that there would be enough of them to do a square eight and have someone playing the fiddle. They went from

107. Georges Arsenault Collection, ms. 258.

108. CEA, Lauraine Léger Collection, Recording 2120.

house to house. I really enjoyed square-dancing. I danced with the Mi-Carêmes even though I wasn't disguised. That was the aim of it. To square-dance."[109]

With the help of alcohol, the masqueraders became more animated as the evening progressed. This was not because they were given a drink at every house. It is important to remember that, in the past, the consumption of alcohol was severely condemned by the priests and that many families were enrolled in the temperance movement. Nevertheless, young men who for the most part had given up alcohol for Lent, made sure they had a supply of liquor for Mi-Carême. Jude Avery recalls that the parish priest in Larrys River, Nova Scotia, preached strict observance during the Lenten period, but that he seemed to "turn a blind eye" and tolerate the presence of liquor on Mi-Carême. The next day, with bottles and jugs emptied, penance began again and lasted until Easter.

109. Georges Arsenault Collection, ms. 252.

## They Knocked on the Porch and on the Door

"One time, our mother told Émile and me to be quiet because the Mi-Carêmes were going to be dropping by that evening. We went upstairs and there were two holes about an inch wide in the floor over the kitchen. So we took a line and a hook to try and take off one of the Mi-Carême's mask to see if they were real Mi-Carêmes. We thought Mi-Carêmes really existed. In any case, we heard them coming with their bells. They started dancing in the kitchen. We lowered the hook and got one by the mask. We lifted his mask up and wasn't it Anselme Chiasson! He wasn't pleased. When he came upstairs, we told him that we knew we'd catch one, that they weren't real Mi-Carêmes, they were just people like us."

— **Frédéric Roussel** (Le Goulet, New Brunswick)

"Us folks in the village of Wellington lived among people of different religions and they had no idea what Mi-Carême was about. For us folks, we thought it was okay for everybody. We even went to the minister's house because it was close. We knocked on the doors and they looked at us: 'What's going on? It's not Halloween yet. What are you doing here?' But they were nice just the same, they gave us whatever they had. They usually gave us cookies or they gave us fudge. Some of them gave us pennies if they didn't have anything else."

— **Monique Arsenault** (Wellington, Prince Edward Island)

"Some families wouldn't let Mi-Carême visitors in. These families said their children were frightened of Mi-Carêmes and that they wouldn't sleep if they saw them. Others were old folks who didn't want to be disturbed. As far as I can remember, we accepted these reasons and went on our way. We didn't like Mi-Carêmes from other areas encroaching on our territory. I don't remember seeing any incidents where this refusal caused any serious problems, perhaps a few scuffles, but nothing more."

— **Fernand Gaudet** (West Collette, New Brunswick)

"I remember Mi-Carême very well. The masqueraders even came around in the daytime. It was wonderful. It was whoever had the nicest outfit. There were some people who died from being a Mi-Carême, they were so exhausted and tired from acting and running around. It's not always nice weather in the winter. They were soaking wet, they got pneumonia, then they died of that. It was the cause of their death."

— **Maria Goyetche** (Petit-de-Grat, Nova Scotia)

"There weren't many. A couple, two or three. It was only old guys that went around at Mi-Carême. You'd never have seen a child or a young fellow making house-visits at Mi-Carême. I remember at my Grandfather Élie's place. He lived to the east of my Uncle Paul. We dropped in there by chance one time during Mi-Carême. Oh, were we ever scared! Were we ever scared! They were parading around with a flaming torch, lanterns, masks of the devil, rifles on their backs. It was frightening. They were banging on pots. We didn't go outside. We were told that the Mi-Carêmes were coming, they were like beasts. It was scary!"

— **Édwidge Landry Carbonneau** (Natashquan, Quebec)

"Because there was no outside light at our place, we couldn't see anything. We waited, scared to death. The Mi-Carêmes entered suddenly without invitation. Almost all of them had a big stick that they banged on the porch and on the door and then they spread out all over the room. One person in the group would often agree to uncover his face when it was obvious that the young ones were really frightened."

— **Edmond A. Bourgeois** (Grande-Digue, New Brunswick)

"There were some folks who got dressed up at Mi-Carême. I remember some of them came to our place, I was really scared of them. They were disguised. Some of them who came played the fiddle in the kitchen. Mom gave them a treat. Mom laughed, she was a happy person and she liked having fun. I was frightened because it was men who were going around. It wasn't girls or children. Married men and young guys. After that, things were quiet until Easter."

— **Simone Bernard** (Dalhousie, New Brunswick)

"I went around at Mi-Carême, even after I was married. We'd meet at the priest's house and divide up into groups. Each group visited one part of the parish. At some of the houses, they gave us molasses cookies. We'd sing and dance in the houses. We'd end up at Daniel Richard's. We'd get there around midnight. There was a big dance. The girls gathered there to dance with the Mi-Carêmes."

— **Timothée Robichaud** (Leech, New Brunswick)

"Us young girls stayed at home. We were very frightened of the Mi-Carêmes. It was mainly the older guys who put on all different kinds of costumes. I remember one time when I was really scared. Someone was disguised with a bear skin. I really thought it was a bear. Another time, we were going to the prayer that was said every evening in the chapel. When we were leaving the chapel, we saw the Mi-Carêmes coming. We could hear the noise and see them in the distance with their sticks and bells. We were so frightened that we hid under the bridge. We really thought it was the devil in person."

— **Caroline Basque** (Tracadie, New Brunswick)

"On the evening of Mi-Carême, we didn't leave the house after supper because we knew they were going to come and we were scared. So we stayed at home, waiting for the first knock at the door. We heard them coming. They were banging their canes everywhere. They were taking their canes and banging them on the doors. I remember my father going to open the door and saying to them, 'Hey there, try not to smash everything.' He let them in, then they lined up against the wall. From time to time they banged their canes on the floor, then they took two or three steps towards us. I remember my father trying to guess who was who. When they went away, they left traces behind. The next morning, we went outside and found bits of ribbon, pieces of rags, and even torn clothing. They'd been fooling around amongst themselves, we found all that stuff along the road, in the back yard."

— **Diane Thébeau** (Saint-Ignace, New Brunswick)

# Singing, Dancing, and Fighting

The customs related to Mi-Carême have changed considerably over the years, although the lack of documents makes it difficult to track the changes, especially prior to the twentieth century. It is obvious, however, that the practices on this festive day did not evolve in the same way everywhere. In some Acadian areas, making house-visits on Mi-Carême was restricted to a single group of men who went around their village, whereas in others, women and children also participated in the masquerade. Thus, throughout the day, people would welcome not just one group of revellers into their homes, but many small groups and even solitary masqueraders.

Evidence collected on the Magdalen Islands and on the Gaspé Peninsula indicates that in some villages in the nineteenth and early twentieth centuries, only one man in a group of men would be dressed as a Mi-Carême. According to Father Anselme Chiasson's informants on the Magdalen Islands, "One group was organized in each district and only one person in the gang wore a costume and a mask. The others accompanied this person from house to house. Along the way, new recruits would join the troupe that gradually became bigger."[110] The ethnologist Carmen Roy provides a more detailed description of a similar tradition among the Acadians of Chaleur Bay on the Gaspé Peninsula:

> In that part of Chaleur Bay, a single person, of the male persuasion, symbolized Mi-Carême. However, a Mi-Carême

110. Father Anselme Chiasson, *Les îles de la Madeleine. Vie matérielle et sociale,* Montreal: Leméac, 1981, pp. 150–1.

> was chosen for each of the two ends of the village and taken on a sleigh through all the streets. Whenever the two Mi-Carêmes and their followers met, it would occasion simulated battles with bashing of sticks, shouting, and considerable noise. After these demonstrations had lasted long enough in the street, the revellers would go into the houses to collect sugar and introduce the Mi-Carême to those who had not participated in the outdoor festivities, and the evening ended with making and then eating taffy.[111]

Sometimes the single Mi-Carême on the Gaspé Peninsula wore a bear skin. At other times, he put on old clothes, then he was covered from head to toe with molasses and rolled in feathers! Carmen Roy points out in her article that the tradition of a single Mi-Carême disappeared around 1910 and was replaced by groups of costumed individuals. The feathered disguise also existed at one time in Natashquan, on the North Shore of Quebec.[112]

As was done in a number of Acadian areas for the Candelmas food collection on 2 February, these groups of men went from door to door under the command of a leader. This is mentioned in the oldest known description of the rounds made by Acadian Mi-Carêmes, published in 1888 by Father Philias F. Bourgeois (see p. 27). The leader played an essential role since he was responsible for the good behaviour of a group of revellers which included at least a dozen men, if not many more. In the Tracadie region of New Brunswick, the leader wore a policeman's uniform, as Alvina Brideau explains:

> There was always a man dressed as a policeman. He didn't wear a mask, he was the one who went up to the house. He'd ask whether they wanted to let the Mi-Carêmes in. Noré was often the one in the policeman's rig. We made a suit for Noré. It was navy blue with yellow stripes sewn on the shoulders and on the trousers. We even made big but-

111. Carmen Roy, *loc. cit.*, p. 95.

112. Pierre Dunnigan and Francine Saint-Laurent, *op. cit.*, p. 27.

tons for his coat. They were all covered with silver foil. Then there was his cap. We made a square cap, like a policeman's cap with a visor.[113]

After he had been given permission to let his troupe enter the house, the policemen would blow a whistle or a horn of some kind to signal to the Mi-Carêmes that they could advance. When they were inside, they would start to dance to the tune of a nonsense song such as:

| | |
|---|---|
| Allons djombo,<br>allons djombo, | Let's go djombo,<br>let's go djombo, |
| Titr' à la ri tomme,<br>à la ri tomme tomme to | Titr' a la ree tomme,<br>a la ree tomme tomme toe |
| Allons djombo,<br>allons djombo, | Let's go djombo,<br>let's go djombo, |
| La femme à Jim à Jos | The wife of Joe's son Jim |
| La ri tomme tomme to.[114] | La ree tomme tomme toe. |

In several villages in the Tracadie region, two of the Mi-Carêmes symbolized a couple who were simply called "the old man and the old woman." Onésiphore Basque remembers that this couple did a little dance that involved crossing their sticks. While they performed, the leader sang a ditty called *Ma tante Maligné*:

| | |
|---|---|
| Ma tante Maligné,<br>ma tante Malonmal, | My Aunt Maligné,<br>my Aunt Malonmal, |
| Ma tante Maligné,<br>elle a pas encore soupé. | My Aunt Maligné<br>hasn't had her supper. |
| La tcheue y traînait,<br>la tcheue y traînait | She was draggin' her ass,<br>draggin' her ass |

113. AFEUL, Bouthillier-Labrie Collection, Recording 3814.

114. AFEUL, Bouthillier-Labrie Collection, Recording 3813. Sung by Alvina Brideau.

| | |
|---|---|
| La tcheue y traînait,<br>et c'était là ma joie.[115] | She was draggin' her ass,<br>and that was my joy. |

The repertoire of the Mi-Carêmes in the Tracadie region appears to have varied from one village to the next. According to Henri Sonier, from Sheila, the songs were quite short: "The songs weren't long because you didn't stay long in the houses, because you had a lot of houses to visit."[116] He learned the one Frank Sylvestre McGraw used to sing:

| | |
|---|---|
| Ma tant' Malenmal<br>et ma tant' Maligné | My Aunt Malenmal<br>and my Aunt Maligné |
| C'est ma tant' Malenmal | It's my Aunt Malenmal |
| Elle n'a pas encore dansé. | She hasn't danced yet. |
| C'est l'monsieur l'Nengar<br>qui va la faire danser | It's Mister Nengar<br>who'll make her dance |
| C'est croyé, croyé, croya, | It's croyeh, croyeh, croya |
| C'est l'monsieur l'Nengar<br>qui va la faire danser. | It's Mister Nengar<br>who'll make her dance. |
| Ma tant' Malenmal<br>et ma tant' Maligné | My Aunt Malenmal<br>and my Aunt Maligné |
| C'est ma tant' Malenmal<br>et ma tant' Maligné | It's my Aunt Malenmal<br>and my Aunt Maligné |
| Qui n'a pas encore dîné. | Who hasn't had her dinner. |
| Ah, c'est l'monsieur l'Nengar,<br>croyé, croyé, croya, | It's Mister Nengar,<br>croyeh, croyeh, croya |
| C'est l'monsieur l'Nengar<br>qui, lui, va l'emporter.[117] | It's Mister Nengar<br>who'll take her away. |

115. AFEUL, Bouthillier-Labrie Collection, Recording 2706. Sung by Onésiphore Basque.

116. AFEUL, Bouthillier-Labrie Collection, Recording 1803.

117. AFEUL, Bouthillier-Labrie Collection, Recording 1804.

## Allons djombo

## Ma tante Malignée

## Ma tant' Malenmal

In the same part of New Brunswick, the Mi-Carêmes in some villages also did a mime dance called "Shave the Black Man" in every house they visited. It was performed by two members of the group: one played the barber and the other played the Black Man. The latter would sit on a chair and the barber would pretend to shave him while step-dancing.

Apollinaire McLaughlin describes this pantomime in the following way: "He put a thing [towel] around his neck, then he pretended to shave him. He put on the shaving cream, then he flicked a sort of knife, pretending to take a little off. He was dancing while he did all that. He had to dance around him. He'd shave a bit, then he'd dance again."[118] Well-known in Quebec, this mime dance used to be part of the entertainment in lumber camps where a great many Acadians worked.[119]

In the regions where one troupe of Mi-Carêmes went visiting in a designated area, it was not appreciated when a neighbouring troupe encroached on another's territory. This appears to have been a fairly common occurrence that resulted in a real battle. "When a group from Tracadie met a group from Rivière-du-Portage," says Sylvio Gareau, "there were huge fights."[120] Léontine Kelly adds further details: "In Tracadie, in Sheila, and then over by Rivière-à-Truites, they got all their Mi-Carêmes decked out in each of those places. Then if they met, they'd fight, and I'm telling you, they defended themselves! I don't know why, but they didn't like each other because they were from different places."[121] As Carmen Roy indicates, similar altercations occurred on the Gaspé Peninsula: "Normally, an encounter with another group of Mi-Carêmes always involved spectacular fights. On Ash Wednesday morning, we'd see bits of costumes, old clothes, blood, and broken sticks along the roads."[122] In some regions, these fights between Mi-Carêmes seem to have been part of the fun and games of the festivities.

---

118. CEA, Carole McLaughlin, Recording 19.

119. CEA, Carmen McLaughlin, ms. 27. See the description of this dance in *La danse traditionnelle au Québec* by Robert-Lionel Séguin, Quebec: Presses de l'Université du Québec, 1986, pp. 92–3. According to Séguin, the dance was called "The Barber's Dance" and was the best-known and most performed of all the gesture dances in Quebec: "It was generally performed on Saturday nights in lumber camps." See also Jeanne Pomerleau, *op. cit.*, p. 398.

120. CEA, Jean-Claude Dupont Collection, ms. 45.

121. CEA, Ronald Labelle Collection, Recording 548.

122. Carmen Roy, *loc. cit.*, p. 97.

The guys obviously enjoyed challenging their neighbours by intruding on their territory, looking for nothing better than a fight to show their superiority, and perhaps more specifically to settle a score. Needless to say, the victims of the invasion were forced to retaliate in order to protect their honour and especially to prevent "strangers" from flirting with the girls in the village.

In general, Mi-Carême was not a time for playing tricks, as compared to Halloween. In any case, as noted previously, the leader of the gang was supposed to watch that his friends behaved properly. However, unsupervised Mi-Carêmes sometimes took advantage of the opportunity to play tricks, especially on people who had refused to offer any hospitality. Dora Frenette, from Petit-Rocher, New Brunswick, remembers one trick that involved climbing up on a roof to block the chimney with burlap bags. The smoke eventually filled the house, much to the consternation of the inhabitants.[123] Robert Gaudet says that in Grande-Entrée, on the Magdalen Islands, a group of Mi-Carêmes who wanted to take revenge on a man whose behaviour they disapproved of, put a horse sleigh against the only door of his house. "Imagine when he went to go out. If there'd been a fire, it wouldn't have been funny."[124]

For young men, the Mi-Carême celebrations constituted a highlight in their life. Being part of a group of masqueraders meant that one had entered the world of men. As a former participant in Le Goulet, New Brunswick, expressed it, they were now "real men." Most of the young men were in their twenties, but one normally joined the troupe around the age of seventeen. Behind a mask, guys allowed themselves behaviour that would otherwise not be permitted and that would be deemed unacceptable in any other context. In the words of many former Mi-Carêmes, "We acted like devils for a little while." It was certainly a chance to have a lot of fun.

123. CEA, Chantale Frenette Collection, ms. 2.

124. Georges Arsenault Collection.

## Mi-Carême

*The Mi-Carêmes' visit to the family home is the oldest memory of Fernand Arsenault, former professor at the Université de Moncton. In the following lively and colourful text, he takes us back to the early 1930s when, for the first time in his life, he was confronted with this surprising masquerade. The event takes place in Bonaventure on the Gaspé Peninsula.*

I was playing with my brothers and sisters when, all of a sudden, there was a loud knock on the door. I was startled and I was frightened! Our house seemed to be engulfed by low voices, songs, laughter, and the banging of sticks. It was dark outside. Mom wasn't home. She had gone for supper at a friend's. Where was my father? I had no idea! Suddenly, the back door opened. A herd of cows invaded the big family kitchen where I was. I was sure I was going to be crushed by these huge beasts. Without hesitating, I ran to take shelter in the cupboard where the saucepans were kept. My heart was pounding. I didn't feel at all safe. To make matters worse, I couldn't close the cupboard door.

The little door was ajar and through the crack I could see men's big legs covered in animal skins, long cow tails dragging on the floor, and sticks hammering the beat of songs and dances. Looking over the top of the door, I could distinguish faces that were half-man, half-bull, heads with big horns, strange and very ugly characters. In the midst of all that, my brothers and sisters seemed to be having a wonderful time while I was scared to death. I was convinced they were going to be trampled, if not devoured, by these animals. I started crying my heart out.

Suddenly, someone pulled on the door I was holding with my little hand. My hiding place had been discovered. I thought I was going to die. The door opened and, by some miracle, my mother was standing there with outstretched arms to snatch me from the jaws of death. I was saved. She held me firmly against her body,

*Illustration: Denise Paquette*

covering me with kisses. As happy as could be, she took me over to the monsters, explaining that they were friends and neighbours who had put on disguises to celebrate Mi-Carême. I was still crying, but I already felt much more reassured. Even in my mother's arms, I didn't dare look at these monsters in the face. Guided by my mother's hand around my little hand, I touched their horns, their beards, their masks, and their sticks. Still paralyzed with fear, I took the risk of looking between my fingers; from high up in the safety of my fortress, I could see these strange characters who earlier had appeared like dangerous monsters. Wrapped in my mother's love, the wonderful thing was that the more I looked at them, the nicer and kinder they seemed.

My mother went over to the stove and took a piece of sausage that was writhing with pain in a pan simmering above the flames. Still holding me tightly against her shoulder, she went over to a big bull with powerful horns and showed him the treat. Trustingly, the animal opened its huge mouth and my mother threw in what looked like a big piece of molasses taffy. The beast gave out a bellow, that seemed to come from the bowels of the Earth, and spit out the hot piece of sausage in a sticky vomit right in the face of a big fat pig, while all the other animals burst out laughing. My mother loved playing tricks. Sometimes she was pretty hard on them. As a way of apologizing to her victims, she went and got a large tray of white taffy, cupcakes, and other nice treats that my brothers and sisters distributed to the members of the Mi-Carême troupe.

The festivity lasted as long as there was taffy. They sang, they danced, and they told stories that made everybody laugh! I even saw some big bulls and the big fat pig dancing with my sisters. My mother invited the red and white bull, who was the leader of the gang, to gather up everything that was left on the plates. He put it all in a big bag while the other members of the herd continued celebrating. It was to share with the poor, he said. When they left our house, they headed towards our neighbours' homes. My older brothers had the privilege of accompanying them.

I really think that it was that event, the visit of the Mi-Carêmes, that put me on our planet. It's my first memory. How old was I? I don't know! But, to be able to crawl into the cupboard, I couldn't have been more than two, perhaps three years old! It's true that I have never been very big! I don't think I was unduly traumatized by the troupe of masqueraders bursting into my young life. I can remember it as clearly as if it were yesterday. I know one thing: Mi-Carême has always been an important festivity for me.

For many people, Mi-Carême was one of the most highly anticipated events of the year. "Of all the distractions," writes Francis Savoie, "Mi-Carême was certainly the one that gave the inhabitants of the region the opportunity every year to see one of the funniest and most fantastic spectacles."[125] Because of the alcohol and the masks, this festivity sometimes resulted in lapses of conduct, but the rounds of the "big" Mi-Carêmes from house to house rarely seem to have been condemned by Acadian religious authorities. They were an integral part of life in the community. In fact, they were so popular that children also wanted to participate.

125. Francis Savoie, *L'île de Shippagan. Anecdotes, tours et légendes*, Moncton: Éditions des Aboiteaux, 1967, p. 34.

# Children Join in the Festivities

Although in most Acadian regions, making house-visits at Mi-Carême was once an activity reserved for young men, it gradually became a tradition observed by children and young people of both sexes. It is impossible to say exactly when the change took place. However, it is clear that it did not happen at the same time everywhere. In his history of Chéticamp, published in 1961, Father Anselme Chiasson writes, "Children and young people, mainly boys but also girls, have always made their rounds at Mi-Carême."[126] At the other end of the province, in some villages of St. Mary's Bay, children never adopted this tradition.

Fernand Arsenault recalls that in the village of Bonaventure, on the Gaspé Peninsula, young boys started taking over from men and going out on Mi-Carême around 1936:

> All the time I was in school, between the ages of eight and fifteen, I was the main organizer of Mi-Carême for children. The adults had abandoned the custom. Along with my young neighbours, I decided that it was our turn to have some fun. We started making our masks and costumes right after the Christmas holidays. At Mi-Carême, we visited the houses in our big neighbourhood. [...] We imitated the old people. We sang, we danced, we asked for refreshments and watched out for food that was too hot! We preferred the houses where there were pretty girls.[127]

---

126. Father Anselme Chiasson, *op. cit.*, p. 213.

127. Fernand Arsenault, *op. cit.*

In the 1950s and 1960s when he was growing up, Robert Gaudet went visiting at Mi-Carême in his native village of Grande-Entrée, on the Magdalen Islands. At that time, adults, mainly men, were still making their rounds at Mi-Carême. While they looked forward to being offered some nice beer, the children could hardly wait for the sweets: "We'd knock on the door, then we'd wait for someone to give us something like fudge. That was what we really wanted to get."[128] Before offering the treats, the hosts would try to guess the identity of the masqueraders. At some houses, recalls Robert Gaudet, "We took off our masks almost as soon as we went in, because we wanted to be sure we got our treat."

Diane Nadeau, from L'Étang-du-Nord, started going from house to house at Mi-Carême in the mid-1960s when she was about eight years old. The children in her neighbourhood made their rounds in groups of three or four and at each house they received treats that they ate right then and there. In Nadeau's opinion, that was not the main object of the visit. "For children of that age on the Magdalens, Mi-Carême was not about getting candies or other things, it was a chance for them to get disguised and to impress the grown-ups. The children would set out as soon as school was out (around three-thirty), just visiting their neighbours. The most important thing was not to be recognized, at least not right away."[129] The young masqueraders would be home by no later than seven o'clock, then the teenagers would start their rounds, often travelling several kilometres on foot.

In the Lamèque region of northeastern New Brunswick, children were given permission by their parents to stay out of school on the afternoon of Mi-Carême in order to go visiting. Like the adult masqueraders, they had a leader. He was the one who chose the members of the group, boys for the most part.

---

128. Georges Arsenault Collection.

129. CEA, Diane Nadeau Collection, ms. 3.

**Little Mi-Carêmes in Chéticamp in 1984.** According to Marie-Colombe Robichaud, children in Chéticamp, Nova Scotia, made their rounds after school and at suppertime, but they were home before dark. Then the young people and adults went out on their rounds. (Marie-Colombe Robichaud Collection)

According to Patricia Savoie, "only the bravest [girls] dared go out because in some houses, there were mischievous guys who enjoyed unmasking or scaring the girls."[130] She also points out that the costumes at Mi-Carême were not as fancy as the ones for the masquerade on Mardi Gras, the eve of Lent, which took place in her region. At Mi-Carême, children would put on old clothes and walk with a cane. Imitating the grown-ups, some of them would even have a pipe they made from a spool and

130. Marielle Boudreau Collection.

a little piece of wood. Patricia Savoie explains that sugar was collected to make candy, as was done on Mardi Gras:

> After we'd finished collecting, we'd go to a house where the mother of one of the children was willing to make taffy or fudge that we'd eat during the evening while we were having fun. If we didn't eat all the taffy and the fudge, it was divided up and each person took home his share. But you weren't allowed to touch it during the week, you had to wait until Sunday, because Sundays weren't included in the forty days of Lent.

In the village of Collette, in southeast New Brunswick, it was children between the age of six and thirteen, and not adults, who went visiting on Mi-Carême in the 1950s until the mid-1960s when the tradition eventually died out. Nicole Maillet Gionet remembers that Mi-Carême was "like a little Christmas,"[131] which they really looked forward to, because it was the only day in Lent when they were allowed to eat a few sweets. People would give them fudge, taffy, or apples. In the Maillet family, she recalls, "We didn't particularly like getting apples unless they were from the store, because we had lots of apple trees out in the yard!"

On Prince Edward Island, where the custom of the mythical Mi-Carême, distributor of treats, was honoured in most of the Acadian areas, it was only in the Evangeline region where there were also masqueraders who went around in groups, a tradition that lasted until the end of the 1960s. The fact that it was predominantly children and young people who were involved would suggest that this custom was introduced in later years.[132] It is interesting to note that even up until the 1950s, both of these customs existed at the same time.

---

131. Georges Arsenault Collection, ms. 276.

132. The Candlemas collection, which took place on 2 February, was very popular in the Evangeline region until the 1940s. It was only done by men, some wearing disguises, who went from door to door under the command of a leader. They would collect food for the poor. See: Georges Arsenault, *Courir la Chandeleur*, *op. cit.* The tradition was revived in 1995. Nowadays, women and children also go out collecting at Candlemas.

**Cute little Mi-Carêmes in Mavilette.** These five little masqueraders let someone take their picture while they were visiting Frank Lézin Boudreau's house in Mavilette in St. Mary's Bay, Nova Scotia, around 1953. The three older children are carrying a stick, the preferred weapon of all Mi-Carêmes. (Université Sainte-Anne Collection)

Born in 1940, Roger Arsenault has happy memories of the years when he went visiting on Mi-Carême in Urbainville, also known as Le Portage. He was seven or eight years old when he started participating in the festivities with his young neighbours and classmates. Most of the people in his village lived on farms so the houses were separated by big fields and, in some cases, they were quite some distance from the road. Consequently, the young Mi-Carêmes took shortcuts to get to their destinations. "If you went by the road, you wouldn't even be able to do half of Le Portage because all the driveways were long, whether it was to Fred's, Alphée Fidèle's, Mic LeClair's, or Jim LeClair's. So we went across the fields. That's how we went from house to house. If there was snow, it was okay, but when there was no snow you climbed over the barbwire and you got your behind caught!"[133]

As Roger Arsenault indicates, they received a particularly warm welcome in the homes where there were no children. "There was Joe's wife Hélène. It was fun to go there. She wanted to know who we were. Before we left to go, we'd take off our masks, then we'd tell her who we were. That made her laugh. We enjoyed that. We'd go mainly to older folks' places. To Fred Jos Martial's, to Jean-Pierre and Angéline's. They loved seeing people in disguises." It was also a pleasure to go to homes where there were musicians. Roger Arsenault remembers that his mother would sit down at the organ and play a reel so the *Mi-Carêmeux*, as she called them, could dance. Like other people, she would reward them with fudge, taffy, or just apples.

Obviously, in many Acadian villages, children, or "little Mi-Carêmes," proved to be enthusiastic participants in the tradition. In some areas, they were even the last custodians. As we shall see, in the places where Mi-Carême is still celebrated, children are always active participants.

---

133. Georges Arsenault Collection.

# The Mi-Carême Soirée

In many villages, the Mi-Carêmes would finish off their rounds with a party that took the form of either a dance or simply a meal for the group who had participated in the masquerade. Fannie Deveau, from Meteghan, Nova Scotia, who was 93 years old in 1980, remembers that when she was young, the masqueraders would end their house-visiting in the inland village of Concession. "There was a house in Concession where they were all invited. They'd take off their outfits and they'd have potato soup, then they'd dance till morning."[134]

The sequence of events was similar in many of the villages in northeastern New Brunswick. In the 1920s, when Aimé Larocque went visiting on Mi-Carême in Saint-Raphaël-sur-Mer, there was a house in the village where the troupe of masqueraders was greeted at the end of the evening. "We'd end up there. They knew we were going to take off our costumes. We got undressed, then we danced for the rest of the evening."[135] Timothée Robichaud, from the village of Leech, near Tracadie, provides a few more details: "We ended up at Daniel Richard's place. We'd get there around midnight. There'd be a big dance. The girls would gather there to dance with the Mi-Carêmes."[136]

It was not always easy to find a house where dancing was permitted. In many Acadian parishes, the priest categorically forbade any activity of that kind. Nevertheless, young people were sometimes able to find a family who was prepared to

134. CEA, Lauraine Léger Collection, Recording 1553.

135. CEA, Lauraine Léger Collection, Recording 2137.

136. CEA, Laurie Robichaud Collection, ms. 15.

defy the prohibition. Such was the case in Bouctouche, New Brunswick, where one house in the Cove welcomed young people on Mi-Carême after they had finished their rounds. Marie-Lucie LeBlanc was too young to attend these gatherings, but she and her friends would peak through the windows to watch the dancers and listen to the lively fiddle music. "We went over and looked in the windows to see what was going on. We had to be back home before a certain time because we had school, and our parents would say, 'Where've you been?' — Just over to see the Mi-Carêmes. We didn't tell them where we'd been in the Cove, because they wouldn't have liked that for sure."[137] The worst thing for these children was that they were obliged to go to confession because they had watched dancers. "We had a priest who was very, very strict and he prohibited dancing. We were already scared enough to go to confession, let alone to have to say we'd looked in the window."

Obviously, not all parents would let their children go to these dances, even if they took place at one of their neighbour's. This was the case for Émilie Melanson, who grew up in Sackville, New Brunswick. "I remember that people in Sackville spent the evening [of Mi-Carême] at my neighbour's house. They had accordions, fiddles, and they danced all evening. I would've liked to go over to that dance, but my parents refused to let us go."[138]

In the regions where children collected sugar during the masquerade at Mi-Carême, they would gather wherever a mother accepted to make fudge or taffy. According to Adolphe Bernard, that is what one did in the Campbellton region of New Brunswick in the early 1900s. "We collected the sugar in bags or pillowcases. Sometimes if people didn't have any, they'd give us money and we'd go and buy some. At the end of the afternoon, all of us kids went to one particular house. The

137. Georges Arsenault Collection.

138. CEA, Monique Goguen Collection, ms. 5.

mother in that house took our sugar and made taffy and fudge. We often played games, like cards, and had fun together."[139]

All parents were not willing to hold this little party in their home, says Fernand Arsenault who grew up in Bonaventure on the Gaspé Peninsula. "My parents, or I should say my mother, refused to let us have the party in our house at Mi-Carême. We weren't allowed to eat any taffy or sweets during this period of fasting and abstinence. However, my mother did let us go celebrate at one of our neighbour's. As for my father, he didn't seem to understand my mother's firm position in this matter. So he kept quiet..."[140] The neighbours, Élide and Claudia Henry, kindly welcomed the gang of young Mi-Carêmes: "We'd throw our costumes and our warm clothes on the floor by the furnace. We'd calculate the contents of the gifts we'd collected and we'd figure out whether we had enough brown sugar to make taffy. If there wasn't enough, Mother Claudia always had some for us. She had the water already boiling on the big wood stove. In no time at all, the taffy was ready to pour on the snow." The young men would spend a good hour singing and stuffing themselves with sweets before going home to bed, because there was school the next day.

For the majority of people, the evening of Mi-Carême was spent welcoming the masqueraders into their homes, getting them to dance, trying to guess their identities, and offering them treats, even a glass of rum or beer. If the evening ended with a party in a designated house, it was more or less reserved for the individuals who had taken part in the masquerade. However, a lot of people liked taking advantage of this day in Lent to enjoy a few pleasures with a clear conscience. They would invite friends over for a game of cards, the fiddle would be taken out of its case, and they would eat a little more meat and definitely more sweets than on the other days in Lent.

---

139. CEA, Diane Bernard Collection, ms. 4.

140. Fernand Arsenault, *op. cit.*.

Fundraising events were even organized in the community in support of good causes. In 1941, the newspaper *L'Évangéline* reported that an event of this kind was held in northeastern New Brunswick. "On Mi-Carême, an evening of Bingo was held at the home of Mr. Euchère Landry to help fund the construction of a school in the upper district of Notre-Dame-des-Érables. Despite the cold temperature, the evening brought in the tidy sum of $26.00."[141] The same year, the residents of Upper Pokemouche gave a concert to mark the occasion. "On Sunday the 23rd [of March] a Mi-Carême concert was held in the parish hall. It was a most successful concert. There were different kinds of music and funny songs followed by some step-dancing. The hall was full. A profit of $58.75 was raised in aid of the church."[142]

141. *L'Évangéline*, 10 April 1941, p. 4.

142. *Ibid.*

# Mi-Carême in Chéticamp and Saint-Joseph-du-Moine

Nowadays, if anyone wants to make house-visits or "run the Mi-Carême" in the Maritime provinces, there is no other alternative but to go to Chéticamp and Saint-Joseph-du-Moine, Nova Scotia. Approximately 4,000 people live in these two parishes on Cape Breton Island. There have always been masqueraders for the Mid-Lent festivities in this well-known part of northern Cape Breton. As Mi-Carême gradually became less celebrated in the 1950s and 1960s in many Acadian villages, it grew in popularity among the Acadians of Chéticamp and Saint-Joseph-du-Moine. Father Anselme Chiasson provides the following testimony in his book on the history and traditions of Chéticamp, published in 1961:

> Today, Mi-Carême is more popular than ever. It has been stretched out from Thursday, the day on which it was once celebrated, to a whole week. Many more people, even adults, participate. Masks are bought at the local store. More elaborate than in the past, the costumes often portray characters such as a policeman, a nun, a nurse, or even Evangeline. The "Mi-Carêmes" travel by car and have expanded their circle of visits. Troupes of amateur singers, dancers, and musicians get together for the occasion and, dressed in disguises, take their merrymaking to as many houses as possible.[143]

143. Father Anselme Chiasson, *Chéticamp. Histoire et traditions acadiennes, op. cit.*, p. 214. See also: *Chéticamp: History and Acadian Traditions*, Wreck Cove: Breton Books, 1998.

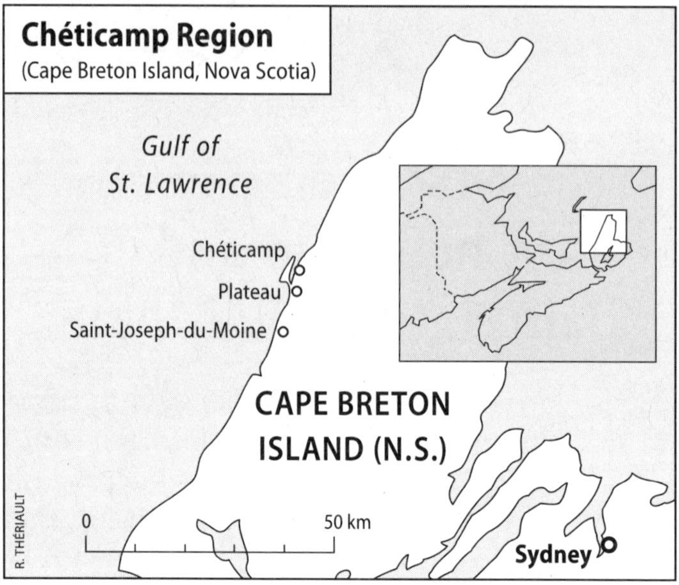


Although Father Chiasson states that by the early 1960s the Mi-Carême celebrations in his native parish lasted a whole week, the vast majority of masqueraders at that time only went visiting on a few evenings. It was not until the early 1990s that Mi-Carême became a week-long festival. Like other young people in her village in the 1960s, Gisèle LeBlanc disguised herself and took part in the masquerade that lasted for three consecutive days. "In my time, it was only three evenings. So we did Chéticamp one evening, Plateau the next evening, then on Friday we did Saint-Joseph-du-Moine." In those days it was still possible to go from house to house on foot because most people welcomed the Mi-Carêmes into their homes. However, over the years, doors were gradually closed. Only the houses that really appreciated these joyful seasonal visitors, the so-called "true Mi-Carême houses," continued to open their doors. Since these hospitable houses were scattered along a stretch of highway about 25 kilometres long, the Mi-Carêmes were forced to make their rounds by car.

LA MI-CARÊME

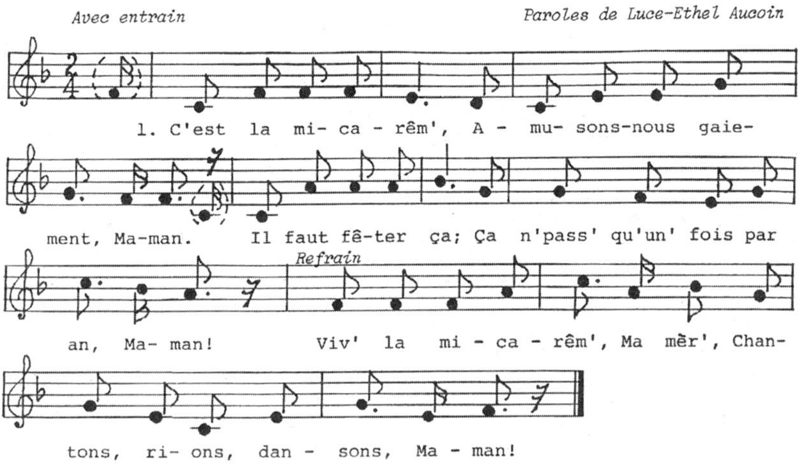


*Lively*

1
C'est la mi-carêm',
Amusons-nous gaiement,
Maman
Il faut fêter ça;
Ça n'pass' qu'un' fois par an,
Maman!

***Refrain***
Viv' la mi-carême,
Ma mèr',
Chantons, rions, dansons,
Maman!

2
On va sous l'église
Se chercher du butin,
Maman.
Les plus distingués
S'habill'nt élégamment,
Maman.

*Words by Luce-Ethel Aucoin*

1
It's Mi-Carême
Let us have lots of fun,
Mama.
We have to celebrate;
It comes but once a year,
Mama!

***Chorus***
Long live Mi-Carême,
My Mother,
Let's sing, laugh, and dance,
Mama!

2
We go down in the church
To get some clothes,
Mama.
The most distinguished
Dress elegantly,
Mama.

| | |
|---|---|
| 3<br>On s'déguise en marié<br>Ou en Soeur du couvent,<br>Maman.<br>D'autr's en policiers<br>Ou Chevaliers d'Colomb,<br>Maman. | 3<br>We dress as a groom<br>Or a Sister from the convent,<br>Mama.<br>Others as policemen<br>Or Knights of Columbus,<br>Mama. |
| 4<br>Yen a qui sont muets<br>Et d'autres très bruyants,<br>Maman.<br>Yen a qui parl'nt anglais<br>Et d'autr's en canadjen,<br>Maman! | 4<br>Some of them are dumb<br>And others are noisy,<br>Mama.<br>Some of them speak in English<br>And others in French Canadian,<br>Mama! |
| 5<br>On sonn' des cloch's à vache<br>Ou des beurgots d'enfant,<br>Maman.<br>Yen a qui sent'nt le musc,<br>D'autr's qui sent'nt la boisson,<br>Maman. | 5<br>We sound the cowbells<br>Or the children's horns,<br>Mama.<br>Some of them smell of musk,<br>And others smell of booze,<br>Mama. |
| 6<br>Yen a qui dans'nt des quatr's<br>Ou bien des rigodons,<br>Maman.<br>Et puis yen a toujours<br>Qui sont bien trop marrons,<br>Maman! | 6<br>Some of them step-dance,<br>Others do the rigadoon,<br>Mama.<br>And some of them<br>Are way too funny,<br>Mama! |
| 7<br>Faut pas abandonner<br>De fêter l'occasion,<br>Maman.<br>C'est comm' ça qu'ça s'pass'<br>Du Moine à Chéticamp,<br>Maman. | 7<br>We can't give up<br>Celebrating this occasion,<br>Mama.<br>That's the way it is<br>From Le Moine to Chéticamp,<br>Mama. |

Song composed in 1987 by Luce-Ethel Aucoin for the first soirée called *Laissons rentrer les Mi-Carêmes*. Source: Daniel Boudreau, *Chansons d'Acadie*, Moncton: Centre d'études acadiennes, Series 11, 2nd Edition, 1996, p. 5.

**You'd like to see some masqueraders? Here are a few!** In 1931, there were lots of young Mi-Carêmes in Chéticamp. Since families were large, it was easy to put together a group of fourteen Mi-Carêmes from only three or four families. This photo was taken by Inez H. MacFarland. (Robert MacFarland Collection)

In 1984, Normand Poirier noticed that in the part of Chéticamp where he lived, only three or four families opened their doors to the masqueraders, in other words about 20 per cent of the households, as opposed to the 80 per cent that had welcomed them in the past.[144] The number of costumed revellers, on the other hand, had not diminished. The decline in the number of Mi-Carême-friendly houses is generally attributed to the fact that modern or modernized houses do not lend themselves very well to this type of activity. People do not wish to see their lovely floors and carpets dirtied or ruined.[145] They are also afraid that their expensive furniture will be damaged by the Mi-Carêmes. Others worry that inebriated Mi-Carêmes will cause a disturbance, which has been known to happen. Finally, it is obvious that opening one's home to hundreds of masqueraders represents an investment in time, money, and energy!

The drop in the number of houses welcoming Mi-Carêmes led people in the community to wonder if the Mi-Carême festivity was not destined to die out. Anxious to maintain this rich and time-honoured tradition, the local committee of the Fédération acadienne de la Nouvelle-Écosse (FANE) decided in 1987 to give this ancient custom a shot in the arm. Charlie Dan Roach provides the following explanation:

> We decided to organize a soirée at the Centre acadien to start the Mi-Carême celebrations on Sunday evening. We called the soirée *Laissons rentrer les Mi-Carêmes* [Let the Mi-Carêmes Come In]. We had dancing and all kinds of music. And we invited people, who weren't prepared to have the Mi-Carêmes in their homes, to come and see them at the Centre. And of course, we invited everyone to wear costumes. We were really surprised, thrilled by the number of people who responded to our invitation. I think there were

144. CEA, Normand Poirier Collection, ms. 1.

145. Réjean Aucoin, "La mi-carême serait-elle en danger de disparaître?" in *Le Courrier de la Nouvelle-Écosse*, 29 March 1979, p. 9.

**Mi-Carêmes are examined carefully.** When a group of masqueraders enter a house, they sit down and wait until the hosts examine them closely, ask them questions, and watch their gestures. Once they are recognized, they take off their masks. These Mi-Carêmes were visiting Robert and Kelly Deveaux's house in Saint-Joseph-du-Moine in 2007. (Georges Arsenault Collection)

**What beautiful eyes you have.** A masquerader is being questioned by Lauraine Aucoin in one of the houses he or she visited in Saint-Joseph-du-Moine in 2007. (Georges Arsenault Collection)

> over 300 people who attended the event, which was a huge success.[146]

Since then, the Mi-Carême soirée, currently organized by the local community radio station, has taken place every year in Chéticamp. It launches the celebrations which come to a close on the following Saturday with the *Gala de la Mi-Carême* in the parish hall in Saint-Joseph-du-Moine. The week-long festivities end with this evening of music and dance which draws numerous masqueraders.

Mi-Carême week has now become an important community event in this region of Cape Breton. The masqueraders are out every day from Sunday to Saturday, making their house-visits in daylight and after dark. The most popular houses greet up to a thousand Mi-Carêmes! Several social clubs also open their doors to these mysterious visitors, as does the Foyer Père Fiset, a senior citizens' home, and the Green Door, a centre for the handicapped.

CKJM, the co-operative radio station in Chéticamp which has been on the air since 1995, has contributed enormously to the festive spirit of Mi-Carême. In addition to playing a lot of old-time music, CKJM frequently broadcasts songs about Mi-Carême composed locally. The homeowners who welcome masqueraders take advantage of CKJM to publicize the dates and times when their doors will be open and to remind the masqueraders that tables laden with refreshments await them. And, just as they do at Christmastime, local businesses have their "Happy Mi-Carême" greetings announced on the radio. The community television station in Chéticamp also contributes to the atmosphere by showing several times during the week various videos on past Mi-Carême parties at the Centre acadien in Chéticamp and in the Saint-Joseph-du-Moine parish hall.

---

146. Radio program on Mi-Carême, part of the series called "Chéticamp," produced in March 2001 by CKJM, the Coopérative Radio Chéticamp.

**Marie-Louise Aucoin and her Mi-Carême friends in 2007.** During Mi-Carême week, Marie-Louise and Paul-Émile Aucoin from Chéticamp receive up to 800 Mi-Carêmes in the basement of their home! Marie-Louise likes a chatty Mi-Carême, but who is not easy to recognize. (Georges Arsenault Collection)

**Musicians at the Centre de la Mi-Carême in 2007.** This Centre, located in Saint-Joseph-du-Moine, is a must not only for many Mi-Carêmes, but also for people who want to see them. There is live music in the afternoons and evenings to encourage the Mi-Carêmes and their admirers to dance. (Georges Arsenault Collection)

Many people in this Acadian region love the Mi-Carême celebrations, although not everyone shares their enthusiasm. An ardent fan of the tradition, Napoléon Chiasson, is aware of this. "For the people who 'run the Mi-Carême' and the people who believe in Mi-Carême, it's certainly a festival. It's fun. But it can be boring for someone who doesn't believe in it, or who doesn't see the sense of it. Those people must take us for a bunch of fools."[147]

Marie-Louise Aucoin, from the village of Plateau in the parish of Chéticamp, is among the really passionate supporters of the festivity. Along with her husband, Paul-Émile, she has been welcoming Mi-Carêmes since 1971. Over 700 masqueraders visit their home every year because they know that they will be well-received and that they will be able to eat their fill. On occasion, these nocturnal visitors have even had their breakfast at the Aucoins before going home in the morning! With the help of the members of her extended family and several friends, Marie-Louise not only makes fudge and cookies for the masqueraders, but also a wide variety of other dishes including chicken fricot, lasagna, chicken and rice casseroles, and even fried eel. As Marie-Louise explains, Mi-Carême is her favourite festivity of the year: "For me, Christmastime drags on forever. But it's different with Mi-Carême. When Christmas is over, people start saying, 'Marie-Louise, take heart, Mi-Carême's coming.' In February, we start thinking about the food we'll serve."

For many years, the Aucoins received the Mi-Carêmes in their kitchen. Eventually, it became too small for the number of visitors. So they decided to do like most of the other householders that welcome the Mi-Carêmes: use their garage or their basement. As Marie-Louise says, at first she was uncomfortable at the idea of breaking with the tradition of greeting people in the kitchen:

---

147. Radio program on Mi-Carême, March 2001, *op. cit.*

> One evening, my husband said to me: "We should let them in the basement." I felt it'd be like sticking the Mi-Carêmes down in the basement! I just didn't feel good about it. I started talking about it with my friends, my family, my brothers-in-law, and my sisters-in-law. They said to me: "Why not? Everyone else has them in the basement." It doesn't bother me now. I wouldn't want the Mi-Carêmes upstairs. No, there'd be too many of them. The basement's perfect.[148]

Marie-Louise and Paul-Émile Aucoin's large finished basement can easily accommodate fifty people. They welcome the Mi-Carêmes from Sunday to Friday, always surrounded by numerous friends and relatives who come to watch the merry-making or to help identify the masqueraders. The stereo system provides background music, but from time to time a group of masked musicians suddenly appear, filling the basement with lively music for ten minutes or so. Marie-Louise walks joyfully about the room, interrogating the Mi-Carêmes, dancing with them, and taking pictures of them, all the while checking that nothing is missing in the way of food. Obviously, she loves these masked visitors. She makes sure they are well-received, even at four o'clock in the morning, because she wants them to come back the next year.

Géraldine Aucoin, from Saint-Joseph-du-Moine, is also a real enthusiast of Mi-Carême. She appreciates enormously people such as Marie-Louise Aucoin, who welcome the masqueraders: "People who let the Mi-Carêmes into their homes are people who want them. They definitely want them, that's for sure. They broadcast it, they expect you. It's really, really fun."[149] Ever since she has had a full-time job, Géraldine takes a week of her annual holidays during Mi-Carême, which enables her to participate in the masquerade every day of the week, sometimes even more than once a day. "It's relaxing, it's real

148. Georges Arsenault Collection.

149. Georges Arsenault Collection.

medicine, it's fun," she exclaims. In 2006, she went out eleven times in ten different costumes! Although she sometimes gets her young son to accompany her, she likes to vary the individuals with whom she makes her rounds because, as she explains, the pleasure is never the same and there are often surprises.

Géraldine Aucoin has Mi-Carême on her mind all year long. When she has to go to Sydney or Halifax, she always makes the rounds of the second-hand clothing stores. She stocks up on used clothing for the next Mi-Carême, because she has to replenish her collection of costumes every year. She has gradually built up a whole wardrobe so that she can now rent costumes and masks for a reasonable price, thus rendering a service to other people in the community and at the same time making a little money, some of which is used to purchase new costumes.

Since 1998, in this part of Cape Breton, there is even a Centre de la Mi-Carême, an initiative of the Le Moine Development Association. Built originally as an attraction to show and explain the Mi-Carême tradition to tourists, the Centre was also developed in order to create jobs in an area hard hit by the cod fishery moratorium. In particular, the Centre provides training aimed at developing a small local industry for the production of masks and other souvenirs related to Mi-Carême. The project co-ordinator, Monique Aucoin, says the Centre de la Mi-Carême is intended to do more than just generate jobs. She sees it as a place that will help promote awareness of Acadian traditions outside Cape Breton, thus strengthening the local pride in Acadian culture and creating significant economic spin-offs. The Centre de la Mi-Carême is open all year-round so it is able to serve as an essential gathering place and venue for activities during the week-long Mi-Carême festivities.

It is obvious that Mi-Carême is not about to disappear in Chéticamp or Saint-Joseph-du-Moine. It runs in the blood. Every year, many Acadians, from as far away as Ontario and

Massachusetts, return to their native region for the festivities. Sometimes they arrive by bus, armed with their musical instruments, costumes, and flasks of liquor, much to the delight of local residents who are happy to see their relatives again for this joyful time of year. Mi-Carême is well-anchored in the community, but that does not mean that it cannot be altered. Many aspects of the celebrations have changed since the 1950s and there will no doubt be other changes in the future. Some people are concerned, for example, that someday there may not be any private homes willing to receive the Mi-Carêmes. If that happens, the masqueraders will have to fall back on community centres, clubs, and, of course, the Centre de la Mi-Carême! With regard to the actual tradition of going out masquerading, Charlie Dan Roach remains very optimistic: "As for going out on Mi-Carême, I don't think there will be a problem, because there are a whole lot of young people who 'run the Mi-Carême.' There are young people who get disguised in three or four different costumes a night. They're really into the spirit of it all. I think we can feel confident that it's going to continue from that point of view."[150]

150. Georges Arsenault Collection.

# Mi-Carême in Fatima on the Magdalen Islands

Mi-Carême was still celebrated in the 1960s and 1970s in most of the villages on the Magdalen Islands, an archipelago belonging to the province of Quebec. Nowadays, the tradition has only been kept up in the parish of Fatima, on the Island of Cap-aux-Meules. As in Chéticamp and Saint-Joseph-du-Moine, it has gradually developed into a community festival. These Acadian communities on the Gulf of St. Lawrence share not only an attachment to this ancient tradition, but also a common history. In fact, many of the founding families in Fatima came from the Chéticamp region between 1825 and 1865.[151] Originally called Barachois, the parish of Fatima includes five districts with a total population of approximately 2,700.

For as long as people can remember, Mi-Carême has always been a popular festivity. In the early 1950s, masqueraders were even welcomed in the parish hall, as evidenced by comments in the newsletter called *La Boussole*: "For several years, the 'Mi-Carêmes' have been gathering in the parish hall in Fatima and claim to be natives of 'Corps-Mort.'[152] Nearly four hundred people flocked to see their fellow citizens who, although strangely dressed and oddly behaved, were most interesting."[153]

---

151. *Barachois-Fatima 1959–1984* (Album for the 25th Anniversary of the Municipality), Fatima, Magdalen Islands: Comité du 25e, 1984, pp. 27–52.
152. The name of a rock off the Magdalen Islands, meaning "Dead Body."
153. *La Boussole*, 1 April 1954, p. 6.

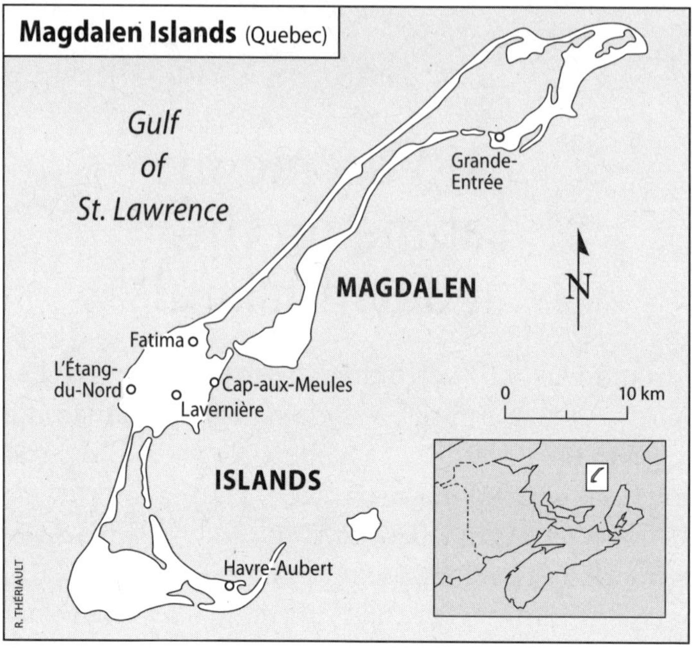


Over the years, not only the number of householders willing to host masqueraders, but also the number of masqueraders, began to diminish. Mi-Carême was obviously fading. To reinvigorate the tradition, the Fatima recreation committee decided to turn it into a festival. An organizing committee was established and the first Festival de la Mi-Carême took place in 2002. The experiment proved to be a great success. Large numbers of Mi-Carêmes turned up in this attractive part of the archipelago where they found many hospitable families happy to receive them. Although the committee organizes various events throughout the week (for example, a play, card games, and a giant bingo), making the rounds of the houses is the highlight from Wednesday to Friday evening. In 2007, about forty houses opened their doors to the Mi-Carêmes. The masqueraders can easily spot the homes that are ready for them, thanks to welcome signs and strings of Christmas lights decorating the houses and the front yards. The Mi-Carêmes can even obtain the program of the festival giving the list of the welcoming houses along with their visiting hours.

**Where's the beer?** These Mi-Carêmes in Fatima look as if there were waiting impatiently for their beer. But they will not be rewarded until they take off their masks. (Michelle Deraspe Collection)

**A noisy entrance.** The arrival of Mi-Carêmes is always noisy in Fatima. Their loud screeches certainly add to the festive atmosphere. (Michelle Deraspe Collection)

In many of these homes the masqueraders are greeted in the kitchen, although precautions are taken to protect the floor. With cardboard covering the entire floor, the Mi-Carêmes can walk freely about the room in their snow boots. Some families prefer to rent a hall for the masquerade. They make sure the space is small enough so as to keep the cozy atmosphere of a kitchen.

As in Chéticamp, the hosts do everything they can to see that the Mi-Carêmes are well-received and rewarded for their visit. They are given the traditional treat of fudge or taffy, along with various types of snacks, sandwiches, and desserts. And, of course, there is always beer, perhaps even some *bagosse* or homebrew. As Isabelle Cummings explains, in partnership with local distributors, the organizing committee of the Festival de la Mi-Carême makes in-kind contributions to the households who welcome the masqueraders: "We give a case of beer, two bags of potato chips, and some pop to each house that receives the Mi-Carêmes. It's automatic, it's free. It's a little incentive to encourage them from year to year because we know it's expensive to have the Mi-Carêmes."[154] Generally, the hosts can count on the help of their close relatives, as is the case at Isabelle Cummings':

> I invite my family, my uncles, my aunts, my grandparents, and my parents. To start off with, there're about 20 or 25 of us in the house. And the condition is that each person brings a case of beer for the Mi-Carêmes and, in addition, each person brings their own drinks for the evening. And the women make the sandwiches, we buy all kinds of little things, so we can have a nice spread for each gang of Mi-Carêmes that arrives, we treat them. That's how it works.

Opening up one's house involves a major commitment and a lot of work. However, neither Gilbert Chevarie's family nor the Cummings family minds because they are ardent support-

154. Georges Arsenault Collection.

ers of the festivity: "We've always loved Mi-Carême. It's in our blood. We were born with it. I'm 40 years old now and I've enjoyed it since I was five. When Mid-Lent comes, we can't help it. It's an addiction!" As the Chevaries know well, it is not just a question of letting the masqueraders in, you also have to give them a good reception: "To let a thousand people in the house over three days, that's some crowd! A lot of people say we're crazy, that we're obsessed. We love it, but you have to prepare. You have to serve them food and drinks. You have to welcome them. You can't have people coming into your home and not take care of them!"[155]

Since it is against the law nowadays to drink and drive, the masqueraders are much more sensible and prudent than in the past. They know they will be consuming more than one bottle of beer during their rounds, so they travel in minivans driven by designated drivers who refrain from drinking any alcohol. Besides, the police increase their patrols during these festive days and encourage drivers to be extra cautious. They warn people to watch out for the hordes of masqueraders wandering the streets of Fatima until late at night. In one evening alone, the most popular houses receive up to five hundred Mi-Carêmes. They are carefully counted. Their numbers have even become the object of an unofficial competition between host houses and the topic of conversation for quite some time after the visitors have left. "When it's all over," relates Isabelle Cummings, "and you go to the grocery store or anywhere else, people are still talking about it: 'Did you receive any? How many did you have?' — Two hundred! — Oh, I had four hundred!' There's a bit of a competition. It's funny."

Mi-Carêmes all love music. Consequently, they are attracted to houses where they know they can hop around for a while to the tunes of some of the famous musicians from the Magdalens. The fiddler Bertrand Deraspe, for example, rarely misses

155. Comments taken from the film *La Mi-Carême* by Éli Laliberté and Patrick Guité, Mimaji Productions, 2006.

**Talented Mi-Carêmes.** In Fatima, a number of Mi-Carêmes make their rounds armed with their musical instruments. These three guitarists had their picture taken during one of their house-visits in 2007. (Michelle Deraspe Collection)

Mi-Carême. On Friday evening, he goes to Gérard LeBlanc's place with several of his musician friends in order to entertain the visitors until the wee hours of the morning. Bertrand also enjoys getting disguised and going from house to house on Wednesday or Thursday evening. He makes his rounds with four other people, also wearing costumes: an accordionist, a guitarist, a singer, and a step-dancer who also serves as presenter. According to the fiddler, "When we go into a house, it makes for a really super atmosphere. It's like an explosion!"[156]

> We go in the house, then we play our first piece, trying not to be recognized too easily. I might play the accordion or the guitar instead of the fiddle. When we really want to be recognized, we play like we usually do. Then it doesn't take them long to recognize us. So we take off our masks and they give us a little glass of homebrew.

156. Georges Arsenault Collection.

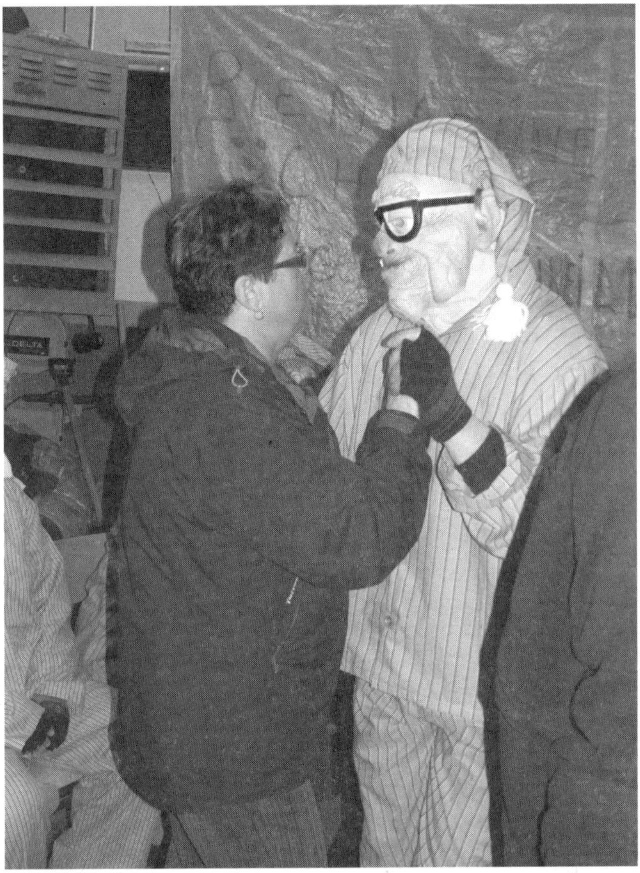

**My, you dance well, Madeleine.** Many houses make sure there are musicians present so the Mi-Carêmes have to dance. Sometimes, it is while they are dancing that they are recognized. (Michelle Deraspe Collection)

After downing their drinks, the joyful troubadours put on their masks and set out for the next house. They try to visit as many homes as possible during the evening, which goes by all too quickly. "If we manage to do about twenty an evening, that's great. We try not to stay any more than 15 minutes." Musicians like Bertrand Deraspe are stimulated by the atmosphere during these festive days: "It's because everyone's really joyful. It's a whole other world. Everybody's in a good mood. People are friendly with each other, and they sing."

Today, Mi-Carême in Fatima is primarily a celebration for adults. However, it is obvious that the future of the tradition will not be secure unless children and young people are included as much as possible. For the past several years, children in kindergarten and in the elementary school in Fatima often have Thursday and Friday off while their teachers attend professional development days. The same is true on Fridays for the one high school on the Magdalens, located in Lavernière. Children and young people can thus enjoy the festival, by taking part in the masquerade themselves or by staying up late to watch the joyful comings and goings of the Mi-Carêmes. In collaboration with the local Optimists' Club, the festival organizers make arrangements so that children can celebrate Mi-Carême on Wednesday from six o'clock to eight o'clock, a time reserved especially for them. With the help of their parents, the little Mi-Carêmes, some armed with their musical instruments, are driven to the ten or so houses that await them. The children go through the same ritual at each house as adult masqueraders: the hosts try to identify them, they play a bit of music, they remove their masks, then they eat.

The community radio helps promote the festival throughout the archipelago, broadcasting special programs or even doing live shows from some of the houses in Fatima hosting the Mi-Carêmes. This media coverage has encouraged people in other communities on the Magdalens to participate in the masquerade.

The inhabitants of Fatima are justifiably proud of "their" Mi-Carême, especially since they are the only ones on the Magdalen Islands, and one of the rare communities in Canada, to have preserved it. Although the lifestyle has changed enormously on the islands since the 1960s, people are still very attached to this ancient tradition. Isabelle Cummings is con-

**A gang of pirates.** In Fatima, as in Chéticamp and Natashquan, a group of Mi-Carêmes often go house-visiting together wearing costumes related to the same theme. (Michelle Deraspe Collection)

vinced that the Mi-Carême festivity still has a place, even in today's modern society:

> It's such a wonderful tradition. People probably don't observe Lent like they used to, but it still gives us the opportunity to take a break during the winter. Even though we live far away from urban centres, even though the quality of our life is good, we still live in a society where we're always running around, where there's always stress, we work a lot, and we have less time to visit our neighbours. So it's nice to have a little break for three days. People visit each other, people take the time to get back in touch with each other, to renew friendships. That's really important.

For some people, like Damien Déraspe, Mi-Carême is like a balm that soothes the community: "What I like about Mi-Carême, is that everybody forgets their little problems. They're put aside. Sometimes, there's a bit of friction between people, but it's forgotten."[157] In the final analysis, it is clear that the Mi-Carême festivity is firmly anchored in Fatima. Only a strong offshore wind could shake its stability.

157. Quote taken from the film *La Mi-Carême, op. cit.*

# Celebrating Mi-Carême in Natashquan and Pointe-Parent

Nowadays, there is no question that Mi-Carêmes prefer places located far away from big cities. Not only that, but they are definitely partial to coastal communities settled by Acadians whose ancestors were victims of the Deportation. In the mid-1800s, Mi-Carêmes must have followed the fishermen and their families who migrated from the Magdalen Islands to the North Shore of the province of Quebec. These Mi-Carêmes obviously adapted well to life in the little villages of Natashquan and Pointe-Parent because, for as long as anyone can remember, they have always reappeared on the fourth Thursday of Lent. The *Macacains* and the *Postons*, as the inhabitants of these two villages are called, were always happy to celebrate Mi-Carême since it provided a welcome break in the long winter isolation, especially before the advent of television in 1974 and the completion of Route 138 in 1996. Natashquan and Pointe-Parent are now linked by this highway to Havre-Saint-Pierre and Sept-Îles, located 150 and 370 kilometres away, respectively.

In a recording made in 1979 of a monologue entitled "La mi-carême," the poet Gilles Vigneault, Natashquan's famous son, talks about the popularity of this tradition that he knew well. In his typically colourful and picturesque language, he evokes the survival of this custom in his native village: "Mi-Carême, is still celebrated at home just as it was in the past. And it's really celebrated! Be careful! Don't confuse this with imitations of a festival or carnival of some kind, like Mardi Gras or Halloween. Those things are not Mi-Carême. Mi-Carême

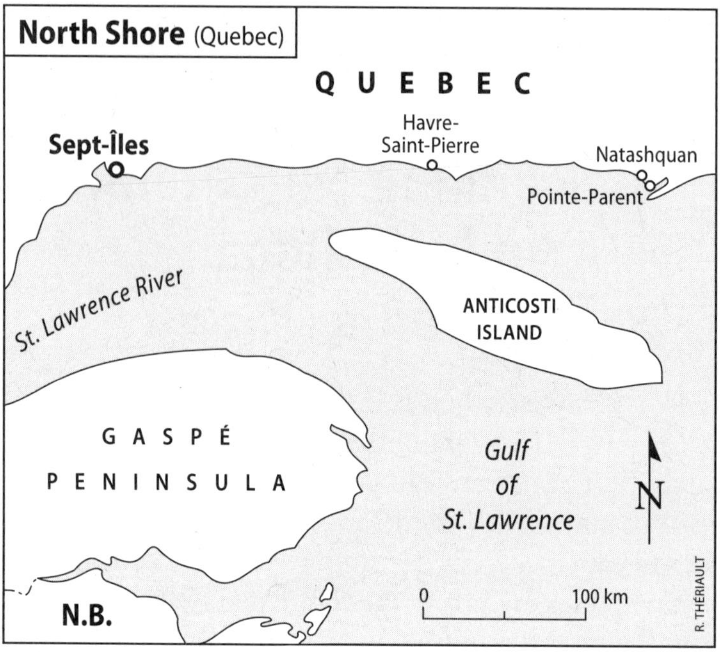


is in the middle of Lent. We've lost Lent, but we've kept the middle! That's true."[158]

As elsewhere, the Mi-Carême masquerade was once reserved for men only in this little Acadie in Quebec. Jean-Charles Landry, who was born in 1918, confirms that it was mainly men who went from house to house during his childhood. "There were never women dressed as Mi-Carêmes in those days. You didn't see little boys going out either."[159] The men went around with torches and took pleasure in scaring people, especially children. "You'd open the door and you'd see drunk guys in oilskins, in all kinds of things like burlap bags, sacking, and barge tarp." Gradually throughout the 1930s and 1940s, the custom was opened up to other members of the community

158. Gilles Vigneault, "La mi-carême," *Avec les mots du dimanche*, Le Nordet, 1979, GVN-1011/12.

159. Bérangère Landry Collection.

**Captain Morgan and his ladies.** In the 1950s, the Mi-Carêmes in Natashquan disguised themselves as well-known characters. In 1957, Marc Landry dressed as Captain Morgan, a popular brand of rum. He is flanked by his wife, Angéline Landry (left), and his sister-in-law, Blanche Landry. (Bernard Landry Collection)

who usually wore costumes made from old clothes. Mi-Carême was particularly popular during the 1950s, when, as Yvon Landry explains, costumes became more sophisticated: "Some villagers, who were real buffs of the tradition, started competing with each other for different things that were likely to make the festivity even more popular, like the originality of the costume and the mask that were supposed to match the person or the animal they were pretending to be..."[160]

160. Bernard Landry Fonds.

The first Mi-Carême that Rosaire Landry, from Pointe-Parent, remembers goes back to the 1950s. He still recalls the beautiful costumes his parents wore on that festive evening:

> My parents were getting ready to go to a masked ball in Natashquan. I was probably around five or six. I was in a little bed. I remember that I was crying. My father was disguised as a policeman in a navy blue suit with gold braid. My mother was also in a very nice costume, too. She was the beautiful chocolate maker. Her costume had been made by Mrs. Marie Vigneault, the mother of our great poet, Gilles Vigneault.[161]

According to ethnologist Bérangère Landry, it is perhaps this major transformation with regard to the costumes that saved the Mi-Carême masquerade in her native village.[162] After that, an informal competition developed to see who would have the best costume or the most original idea. As a result, the masqueraders became impersonators with boundless possibilities: they could pretend to be characters from comic strips, personalities from the world of politics and the arts, or they could turn into animals or inanimate objects. Thus, in one evening, a household could receive Mickey Mouse, the Queen of Diamonds, Céline Dion, the premier of the province, and perhaps even His Holiness the Pope! A Mi-Carême might even impersonate someone in the community, quite successfully sometimes, as Yvon Landry recalls: "One year, I remember that someone imitated a woman in the village right down to all her clothes and a mask of her face. The woman in question was so well impersonated that many people wondered if it wasn't her. So you can imagine the reaction of the woman herself!"[163] Clearly people enjoyed putting on an act. As Bérangère Landry says,

161. Georges Arsenault Collection.

162. Bérangère Landry, "La Mi-Carême. Une coutume venue du Moyen-Âge," *Bulletin du Centre de valorisation du patrimoine vivant*, Vol. 2, No. 2, April 1995, p. 5.

163. Bernard Landry Fonds.

**Labinec and Couette-Couette.** Like the adults in Natashquan, the children also like to go out at Mi-Carême dressed as well-known characters. Tobie and Frédérique Landry are disguised as Labinec and Couette-Couette from a popular children's television show in the 1990s. (Bernard Landry Collection)

"Natashquan becomes a stage, the Mi-Carêmes are the players, and the spectators host the Mi-Carêmes."[164]

Rosaire Landry is one of the passionate fans of Mi-Carême on the North Shore. In 1989, when the festivity was showing signs of petering out, he gathered together a group of volunteers to form an organizing committee for the Festival de la

164. Quote taken from the film *Attendez que je vous raconte*, by Alexandra Angers, Télé Québec, 2002.

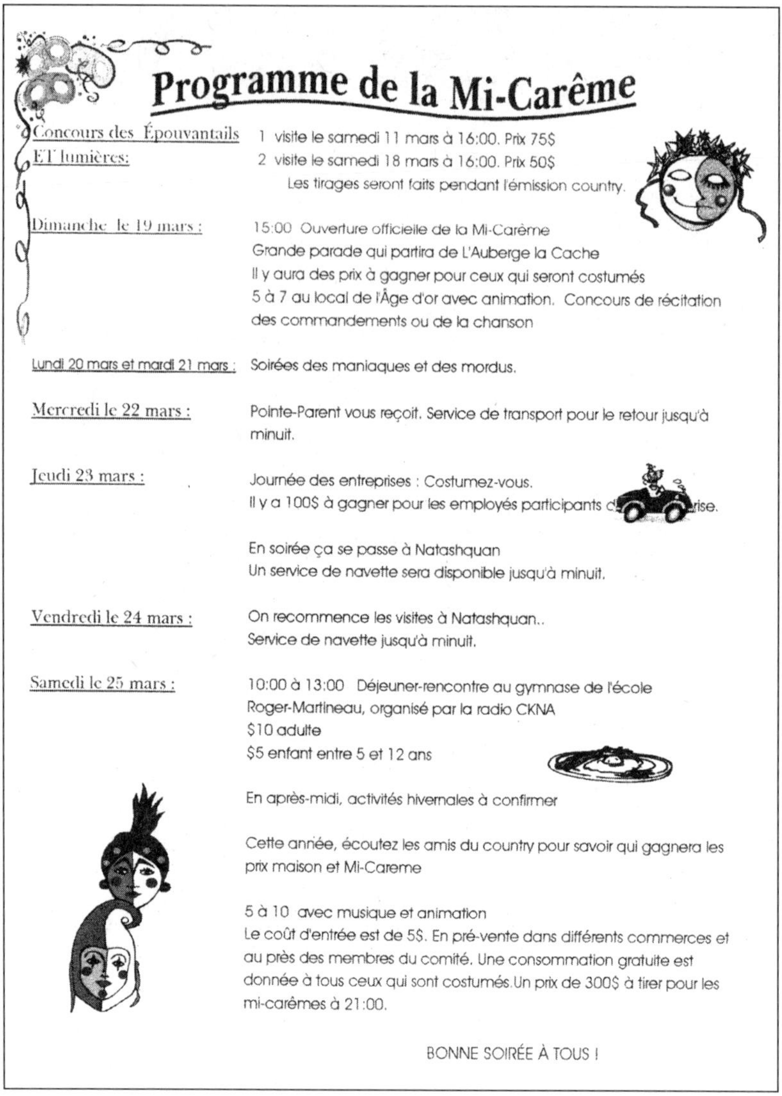

# Programme de la Mi-Carême

Concours des Épouvantails ET lumières : 1 visite le samedi 11 mars à 16:00. Prix 75$
2 visite le samedi 18 mars à 16:00. Prix 50$
Les tirages seront faits pendant l'émission country.

Dimanche le 19 mars : 15:00 Ouverture officielle de la Mi-Carême
Grande parade qui partira de L'Auberge la Cache
Il y aura des prix à gagner pour ceux qui seront costumés
5 à 7 au local de l'Âge d'or avec animation. Concours de récitation des commandements ou de la chanson

Lundi 20 mars et mardi 21 mars : Soirées des maniaques et des mordus.

Mercredi le 22 mars : Pointe-Parent vous reçoit. Service de transport pour le retour jusqu'à minuit.

Jeudi 23 mars : Journée des entreprises : Costumez-vous.
Il y a 100$ à gagner pour les employés participants d rise.

En soirée ça se passe à Natashquan
Un service de navette sera disponible jusqu'à minuit.

Vendredi le 24 mars : On recommence les visites à Natashquan..
Service de navette jusqu'à minuit.

Samedi le 25 mars : 10:00 à 13:00 Déjeuner-rencontre au gymnase de l'école Roger-Martineau, organisé par la radio CKNA
$10 adulte
$5 enfant entre 5 et 12 ans

En après-midi, activités hivernales à confirmer

Cette année, écoutez les amis du country pour savoir qui gagnera les prix maison et Mi-Careme

5 à 10 avec musique et animation
Le coût d'entrée est de 5$. En pré-vente dans différents commerces et au près des membres du comité. Une consommation gratuite est donnée à tous ceux qui sont costumés.Un prix de 300$ à tirer pour les mi-carêmes à 21:00.

BONNE SOIRÉE À TOUS !

The program for Mi-Carême, published in the local newspaper in Natashquan, *Le Portageur,* on 29 March 2006, gives the time and place of the various activities organized throughout the week, beginning with the scarecrow and outdoor lighting competition. There is a parade on Sunday with prizes for costumes, and a recitation competition in the evening. House-visiting takes place in Pointe-Parent on Wednesday and in Natashquan on Thursday and Friday. Employees in the local businesses are invited to wear costumes on Thursday. On Saturday, a meet-and-greet lunch is scheduled from 10 a.m. to 1 p.m. in the high school. The closing party takes place from 5 to 10 p.m., during which prizes are awarded to the Mi-Carêmes.

**No lack of creativity.** The scarecrow competition adds to the festive spirit of Mi-Carême in the village of Natashquan. In 1997, Jean-Charles and Claranda Landry's daughters put together this group, called "Les Épouvantables" (The Dreadfuls).

Mi-Carême. He composed a song inviting his fellow citizens to keep up this precious and unique tradition:

| | |
|---|---|
| Ça r'monte à bien des années | It goes back many years |
| N'faut pas la laisser tomber | We can't drop it |
| La mi-carême,<br>ça s'passe chez nous | Mi-Carême<br>takes place here |
| Rien que chez nous,<br>pis pas partout.[165] | Only here,<br>not everywhere. |

165. Pierre Dunningan and Francine Saint-Laurent, *Mi-Carême, op. cit.*, p. 75.

The first festival took place in 1990, offering a week-long program of activities from Sunday to Saturday. In addition to the traditional house-visits on Wednesday, Thursday, and Friday evening, there are also activities in public halls such as the school gymnasium where all the Mi-Carêmes are invited to gather for the closing event. Attractive prizes are awarded for the most beautiful and the most original costumes. The festival committee encourages people to decorate their houses with outdoor lights. There is also a competition for scarecrows that people put in front of their houses to add to the festive atmosphere of the village. If a house is well-lit and there is a scarecrow, it is a clear indication that the homeowners will open their doors to the masqueraders.

The festival has proven to be a winning formula and has definitely given new life to the tradition of Mi-Carême. Numerous people participate in what has become the event of the year and a magnet attracting the native sons and daughters of Natashquan and Pointe-Parent, now living in Havre-Saint-Pierre, Sept-Îles, and Quebec City. People who once worked in the area also return to take advantage of the opportunity to renew friendships and take part in the masquerade.

Mi-Carême is lived with real intensity in Natashquan and Pointe-Parent, even though their combined population is very small, especially in winter when there are only about 350 inhabitants (excluding the Native population living on the Montagnais Reserve located nearby). About two-thirds of the households welcome the masqueraders and numerous people of all ages wear a disguise. The real fans of the tradition put on their masks at the beginning of the festival, but the house-visits do not usually start until Wednesday when all the Mi-Carêmes go to Pointe-Parent. In 2007, they were welcomed at nine of the fifteen houses inhabited during the winter. Many of them dropped by Rosaire Landry's house, sometimes late at night. "I was one of the houses that had the most during the week. I'm proud to say that I had 82! If a person comes three times the same evening, of course that counts for three Mi-Carêmes because they wear three different costumes." On Thursday and Friday evening, the house-visits take place in Natashquan, where about thirty householders welcome the masqueraders into their kitchens or their living rooms. Children also participate in the festivities. The youngest put on their costumes in the late afternoon, whereas the older ones go from door to door in the evening with their friends or their parents.

People enjoy having the Mi-Carêmes in their homes so they make sure they are well-received. The Mi-Carêmes are always offered a glass of beer, wine, or hard liquor, and are invited to help themselves to the food, as is done in Chéticamp, Saint-Joseph-du-Moine, and Fatima. In comparison with these communities, Natashquan and Pointe-Parent are very small. There are fewer Mi-Carêmes; consequently, they are easier to recognize, but that does not prevent people from enjoying the masquerade. "In a closed environment like Natashquan," says Bérangère Landry, "nothing goes unnoticed. Everybody knows everything, there are no secrets because everybody knows everybody. So it's a chance to be incognito, if only for a few minutes, and no one can resist that luxury."[166]

As is the case in many other villages in Quebec, the Maritimes, and elsewhere in Canada, Natashquan is experiencing an outmigration that not only jeopardizes the future of the community, but also the survival of the Mi-Carême tradition. The lack of jobs has resulted in an exodus of young people and even entire families. Rosaire Landry, a great proponent of Mi-Carême, has himself been affected by this exodus. Both his son and his daughter live far away from the family home. "My children have been gone since the age of 13. That's what I've found the hardest. I don't need to tell you that when they can get time off to come and celebrate Mi-Carême, they're really happy."

---

166. Bérangère Landry, *loc. cit.*, p. 6.

Marie-Claude Vigneault has been making house-visits at Mi-Carême ever since she was child. She does not want to see this ancient tradition disappear because it is so connected to the history and identity of Natashquan. She joined the Mi-Carême committee in order to ensure the survival of this festivity that unites the community so successfully:

> As for me, I love the Mi-Carême festivity, because we forget everything during the week of Mi-Carême. It's as if we fall into a sort of fairyland. We take advantage of it to go visiting, to go see people we don't have time to visit during the year. It's as if we forget all the little disputes of the village, and everybody celebrates together. That's what I hope is going to continue.[167]

Thus Mi-Carêmes need not worry, they will be welcome for a long time to come in Natashquan and Pointe-Parent. People are so proud of them that they have granted them a place in the local museum, Le Bord du Cap, alongside other exhibits on the history of Natashquan.

---

167. Georges Arsenault Collection.

# A Resilient Tradition

Mi-Carême is still a very lively celebration in a number of Acadian communities. As we have seen, it has even been expanded from one day to an entire week in the villages of Chéticamp and Saint-Joseph-du-Moine on the Island of Cape Breton; Fatima on the Magdalen Islands; and Natashquan and Pointe-Parent on the North Shore of Quebec. However, memories of this festivity are fading rapidly in other Acadian areas, especially in New Brunswick and the Gaspé Peninsula. Since the 1940s, the custom of masquerading and making house-visits has steadily declined; consequently few people under the age of fifty have ever seen masqueraders at Mi-Carême.

The Second World War (1939–45) appears to have had a major impact on the Mi-Carême tradition, especially in the regions where masquerading was above all the prerogative of men. After Canada entered the war, many young men, the guardians of the tradition, left their villages to join the armed forces or to move to cities where it was easier to find work in the war industry. After they were gone, fewer people were left to keep up the tradition of the masquerade. However, it was especially during the 1960s that the vitality of Mi-Carême diminished significantly in Acadian communities. After the Second Vatican Council (1962–65), Lent was no longer a period of abstinence and penance; as a result, the festivity at Mi-Carême or Mid-Lent lost its reason for being. The fourth Thursday of Lent soon went by unnoticed and the desire to go out masquerading at Mi-Carême faded as the years passed.

**Don't go so fast.** These Mi-Carêmes making their rounds in the Evangeline region of Prince Edward Island in 1981 travelled on foot and by car. (Georges Arsenault Collection)

Other factors contributed to the decline of the Mi-Carême masquerade. As was the case in a number of parishes in Quebec, priests in a few Acadian villages advised against this form of amusement or even forbade their parishioners to take part in it. In 1939, for example, a parish priest on Isle aux Coudres, in the St. Lawrence River, prohibited masquerading not only because of the risks to one's physical and moral health, but also because Lent was a time of penance when it was compulsory to make "the prescribed sacrifices."[168] On Isle Madame, Nova Scotia, the priests forced their parishioners to move the masquerade from Mi-Carême to Shrovetide, the period before the beginning of Lent, as Joseph-César LeBlanc explains:

> I remember the days when Mi-Carême was an important affair. People would let off steam. It was supposed to be in

168. Serge Gauthier, "La mi-carême dans Charlevoix," *Revue d'histoire de Charlevoix*, No. 35, November 2000, pp. 2–5.

**Posing for posterity.** Mi-Carême was still a popular festivity in West Pubnico, Nova Scotia, in the mid-1950s when this picture was taken. Three of the masqueraders are wearing elegant fur coats. (Centre acadien Collection, Université Sainte-Anne)

> the middle of Lent after people had been fasting for twenty days, so they wanted to unwind completely. But the Acadian priests here managed to have it put before Lent, during the fat days. They transferred Mi-Carême to the days just before the beginning of Lent. There were three days. There was Shrove Sunday, Shrove Monday, and Shrove Tuesday, then penance started, Lent started. So it was arranged the way the priests wanted it, so Mi-Carême took place before Lent. It was still called Mi-Carême, but it wasn't in the middle of Lent.[169]

According to Marie-Victoria David, also from Isle Madame, the priests serving the parish in Petit-de-Grat in the early 1900s put an end to the practice of going from house to house because

169. CEA, Ronald Labelle Collection, Recording 1764.

the masqueraders sometimes caused damage: "Outsiders starting coming and it so happened that they broke things in the houses. The priest stopped it [the masquerade]. In those days, it was Father D'Auteuil, then Father Chouinard.[170] They said people had to stop doing it."[171] Maria Goyèche, another informant from Petit-de-Grat, says that the priests forbade the custom because there "were too many complaints about the booze, it was dangerous."[172]

Ethnologist Carmen Roy states that the religious authorities on the Gaspé Peninsula were more anxious to prohibit Mi-Carêmes from making their rounds because of their disguises and frightening behaviour "that caused the elderly to have seizures, pregnant women to faint or to miscarry, and children, who were terrified of the masks, to have nervous breakdowns."[173]

The practice of masquerading at Halloween, an Irish tradition that became widespread in the United States in the nineteenth century,[174] began appearing in Acadian villages around the 1950s and rapidly became more popular than the Mi-Carême masquerade. People saw so much similarity between the two customs that they sometimes used the word "Mi-Carêmes" when referring to the masqueraders on 31 October. In some families, children were not allowed to take part in a masquerade twice a year. In the presence of the growing popularity of Halloween, considerably strengthened by advertising and commercialization, the masquerade at Mi-Carême lost out.

---

170. Fathers Henri-Joseph Louis de Gonzague Chouinard and Joseph Alphonse d'Auteuil served as parish priests in Petit-de-Grat from 1912 to 1916 and 1916 to 1921, respectively. Both priests were from Rimouski, Quebec. *Paroisse St-Joseph. 100e anniversaire 1904–2004*, [Petit-de-Grat], 2004, pp. 13–14.

171. CEA, Jocelyne Marchand Collection, Recording 514.

172. CEA, Lauraine Léger Collection, Recording 1429.

173. Carmen Roy, *op. cit.*, p. 96.

174. Hélène Dionne, "L'Halloween : carrefour de traditions et de jeux," *Masques et mascarades*, Montreal: Fides/Musée de la civilisation, 1994, pp. 29–51.

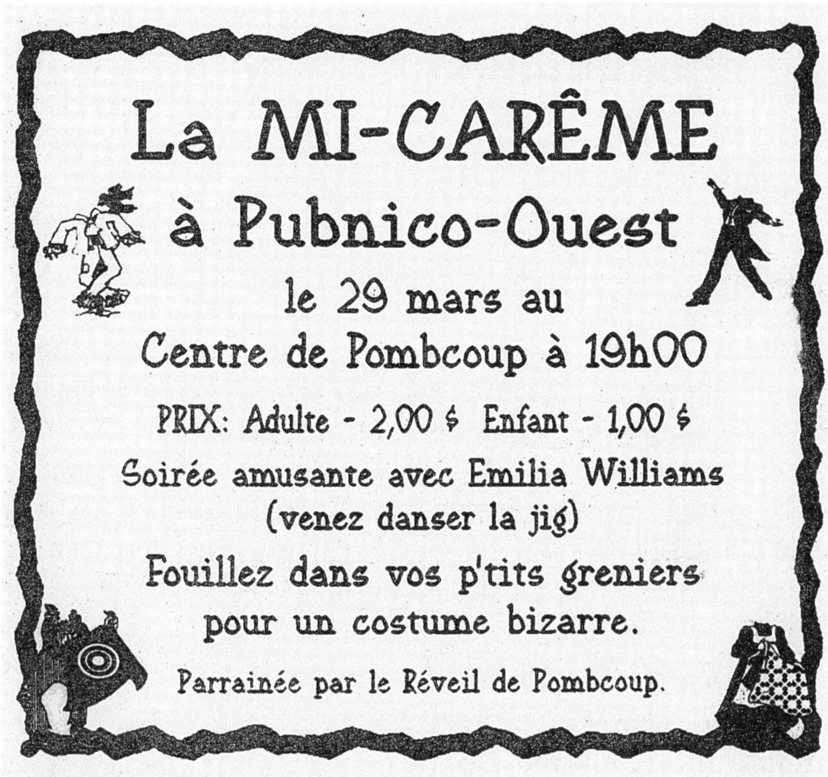


In 1982, the Réveil de Pomcoup, the cultural association in West Pubnico, Nova Scotia, revived the tradition of Mi-Carême, which had died out. Children and adults were encouraged to look in their attic for the makings of a strange costume. Everyone was invited to come for an evening of fun and step-dancing at the Centre de Pombcoup. (*Le Courrier de la Nouvelle-Écosse*, 17 March 1995)

After 1970, a number of attempts to revive the ancient tradition of Mi-Carême were made in several communities in the Maritime provinces; none of them, however, produced lasting results. A more recent initiative took place in the little village of Hubbards Point, Yarmouth County, Nova Scotia. In 2003, the local community centre held its first Mi-Carême soirée. The fifth annual gathering, held in 2007, drew about one hundred people, thirty of whom came in costumes. In accordance with the tradition, the participants were treated to music and refreshments, including fish chowder and rappie pie.[175] Time will tell if the annual habit of socializing and masquerading has become firmly entrenched among the Mi-Carêmes in this corner of Nova Scotia.

In the final analysis, the festivity of Mi-Carême has evolved over the generations. Once celebrated throughout most Acadian regions, its geographical distribution shrank considerably during the twentieth century. Nevertheless, the basic elements of the celebration are still the same: a masquerade, door-to-door visits, hospitality, music, dancing, treats, and even alcoholic beverages. At first, only men "ran the Mi-Carême." Today, people of all ages take part. In the places where Mi-Carême is still a really significant community event, a number of changes have contributed to the resurgence of this ancient festivity. Thus, to ensure its survival and make it more appealing in today's world, the relatively simple festivity that once lasted two days at the most has been transformed into a festival that lasts an entire week and includes a variety of activities.

Despite the vicissitudes it suffered during the twentieth century, Mi-Carême is still celebrated in a number of Acadian communities. To a certain degree, this festivity symbolizes both the resilience of the Acadian people and their attachment to their traditions. For a long time, the character of the Mi-Carême, whether alone or in groups, occupied an important place in the imaginary and social life of the Acadian people. The frightening aspect of the character has gradually been suppressed, exposing above all a jovial and festive personality. In the communities where people are still honoured by the annual visits of one Mi-Carême or many Mi-Carêmes, the character has become a true social animator, a cultural identifier, and an Acadian symbol. Obviously, these Mi-Carêmes are content on Acadian soil and will remain faithful for as long as they are welcomed.

175. *Le Courrier de la Nouvelle-Écosse*, 23 March 2007, p. 32.

**The framed and highlighted oral testimonies throughout this book were taken from the collections of a number of researchers.**

**Collections at the Centre d'études acadiennes, Université de Moncton:**

Georges Arsenault
Lynn Basque
Diane Bernard
Joanne Boudreau
Sophie Daigle
Fernand Gaudet
Michel Laplante
Lauraine Léger
Robert Richard
Laurie Robichaud
Nicole Thibault

**Collection at the Centre acadien, Université Sainte-Anne**

Carmen d'Entremont

**Private Collection**

Bérangère Landry

## Books by Georges Arsenault

*Complaintes acadiennes de l'Île-du-Prince-Édouard.* Montréal: Leméac, 1980.

*Courir la Chandeleur.* Moncton: Éditions d'Acadie, 1982.

*Les Acadiens de l'Île : 1720–1980.* Moncton: Éditions d'Acadie, 1987.

*The Island Acadians: 1720–1980.* Charlottetown: Ragweed Press, 1989. Translated by Sally Ross.

*Par un dimanche au soir : Léah Maddix, chanteuse et conteuse acadienne.* Moncton: Éditions d'Acadie, 1993.

*Guide historique de la région Évangéline.* Moncton: self-published, 1994.

*Historical Guidebook of the Evangeline Region.* Charlottetown: self-published, 1998. Translated by Sally Ross.

*Contes, légendes et chansons de l'Île-du-Prince-Édouard.* Moncton: Éditions d'Acadie, 1998.

*Acadian Legends, Folktales, and Songs from Prince Edward Island.* Charlottetown: The Acorn Press, 2002. Translated by Sally Ross.

*Cent ans de succès / A Century of Success.* Wellington: L'Exposition agricole et le Festival acadien de la région Évangéline, 2002. Translated by Daphne Davey.

*Noël en Acadie.* Tracadie-Sheila, NB: La Grande Marée, 2005.

*Acadian Christmas Traditions.* Charlottetown: The Acorn Press, 2007. Translated by Sally Ross.

*La Mi-Carême en Acadie*. Tracadie-Sheila, NB: La Grande Marée, 2008.

*Acadian Mi-Carême: Masks and Merrymaking*. Charlottetown: The Acorn Press, 2009. Translated by Sally Ross.